Praise for *The Agility Shift*
and Pamela Meyer, PhD

"Pamela Meyer has done it again. This book is a tour de force for leaders at every level who must develop a capacity to experiment, adapt, and learn amidst a turbulent VUCA environment. She offers insight that ranges from neurobiology to relational webs; stories that range from leaders of major corporations to UPS managers; the challenges that range from recruiting agile leaders to creating cultures that nurture them. Covering a wide terrain at such a deep level, this is an important book that deserves a wide readership."

–Frank J. Barrett, author of *Yes to the Mess:*
Surprising Leadership Lessons

"Business is changing at a more rapid pace today than has ever been seen before. *The Agility Shift* offers an insightful view of understanding changing contexts, taking necessary action, and building an ecosystem that makes positive shifts happen. Brilliant yet simple, *The Agility Shift* is a must-read for all professionals and will serve as a useful, practical guide in today's constantly changing business environment."

Rohit Manchanda, Trade & Investment Commissioner, India, New South Wales Government, Mumbai

"Just as I did, you will learn what agility is and how it can work for you and your team in this detailed and highly entertaining road map to the countless benefits of the agility shift. Brimming with compelling examples of agility in action, this is an essential guide to a new and more effective organizational approach."

–Tom Barr, PhD, knowledge manager, Enablon
North America Corp

"This book is a powerful guide to navigating change, especially the unexpected shifts in every industry and market context that call on us to respond more adeptly and meaningfully. It offers leaders, teams, and organizations strategies to enhance their practices, and the courage to discover the opportunity present in every challenge, change, or crisis we encounter in the workplace or in our lives. Dr. Meyer's writing is clear and insightful, with relevant and diverse examples and stories that drive significant points about intentionally transforming organizational life. Without an Agility Shift, there is no path to learning and growth."

—Lisa Gundry, PhD, professor and director, Center for Creativity and Innovation, DePaul University

"Pamela Meyer's new book is a must-read. She brings a unique combination of personal and professional experience and her practical approach and tools can help leaders, individuals, teams, and organizations make the shift to being more responsive, innovative, and agile. I highly recommend this book!"

—Ann Manikas, VP of human resources and inclusion, United Way of Metropolitan Chicago

"Pamela Meyer makes clear in *The Agility Shift* that if we want to survive and thrive (in good times and in crisis), all individuals, teams, and organizations must make a strategic priority of becoming more agile. Just as importantly, she lays out recommendations for how to do it."

—Greg Owen-Boger, coauthor, *The Orderly Conversation: Business Presentations Redefined*

"Meyer's research and experience illustrates that agility is not an option—it is a necessity in order to survive the demands of today's business world. Yesterday's 'comfort zone' is gone, replaced by the challenging 'UNs zone': all that is unplanned, unpredictable, unexpected, and unknown. *The Agility Shift* details how companies can become agile and prepare for the UNs by questioning assumptions, continually learning, being open to trial and error, making incremental decisions, and forming a robust relational web. Meyer provides a powerful framework and accompanying practical suggestions to help you immediately start creating an effective culture of agile leaders and teams. Shift your mindset now, become agile, and find unlimited opportunities in the UNs!"

—DeBorah Lenchard, director of education & talent development, Spot Trading LLC

THE
AGILITY
SHIFT

THE
AGILITY
SHIFT

Creating AGILE
and Effective Leaders,
Teams, and Organizations

PAMELA MEYER

First published by Bibliomotion, Inc.
39 Harvard Street
Brookline, MA 02445
Tel: 617-934-2427
www.bibliomotion.com

Printed in the United States of America

Library of Congress Cataloging-in-Publication Data

Meyer, Pamela.
  The agility shift : creating agile and effective leaders, teams, and organizations / Pamela Meyer.
    pages cm
  Summary: "The Agility Shift shows business leaders exactly how to make the radical mindset and strategy shift necessary to create an agile, entrepreneurial organization that can innovate and thrive in complex, ever-changing contexts"—Provided by publisher.
    ISBN 978-1-62956-070-0 (hardback) — ISBN 978-1-62956-071-7 (ebook) — ISBN 978-1-62956-072-4 (enhanced ebook)
  1. Organizational change. 2. Organizational effectiveness. 3. Strategic planning. 4. Leadership. 5. Management. I. Title.
  HD58.8.M486 2015
  658.4—dc23
                                    2015019129

To all who wish to live and work in the dynamic present moment, where anything is possible.

CONTENTS

PART THREE
Putting Agility to Work

INTRODUCTION

As the team members filed into the workshop I was about to lead, it was clear that they were still digesting what they had just heard. No one knew any details about the just-announced job cuts or about her individual fate, let alone the implications for the team. Months earlier I had been invited to lead this team in what was intended to be a somewhat playful team-building session that left the group (and the organization as a whole) feeling better about their capacity to improvise.

On the day of the session I arrived at the corporate campus early, and as I waiting in the lobby I scanned the business news on my smartphone. My heart started racing as I read a headline announcing that the company that I was about to work with had just that morning reported record losses and announced it would be laying off thousands of workers across the global organization. I then realized that the building I was in seemed like a ghost town. After seemingly endless minutes passed, the human resources director who had engaged me appeared in the lobby. As he walked me back to our session room he let me know that the offices were so quiet because the entire company was in a hastily called town hall meeting with the CEO about the layoffs. But not to worry, he assured me, the team I would be working with had been asked to leave the meeting early and would arrive on time for our long-scheduled learning experience.

I admit my first impulse on the fight, freeze, or flight continuum was flight. Perhaps I could arrange for an urgent call from my nonexistent child's school or be overcome with a mysterious illness.

Rather than give in to my flash of panic, I took a few breaths as we walked the long corridor. I couldn't help but recognize the irony and opportunity. After all, responding effectively to the unexpected and unplanned was the very focus of my work and was one of the main reasons I had been asked to design a workshop for this team. However, my original plan for helping them develop these capacities no longer made sense. That morning, the company's leaders, their countless teams and departments, and the entire global organization found themselves smack in the middle of the unpredictable and unplanned—and, with no notice, I found myself there too. The organization was confronting VUCA (volatility, uncertainty, complexity, and ambiguity), a term now widely used to describe today's business reality. Regardless of the degree to which members of the organization were aware of the gathering storm, it was clear that no one was prepared for its timing or intensity.

As I arrived in the workshop room, I quickly abandoned my original plan and began to regroup and reframe the session objectives and approach. What was originally designed as a lighthearted team-building session quickly became an opportunity for the shell-shocked participants to rediscover their own individual and team capacities to be agile in a very stressful situation.

After acknowledging the current reality and the uncertainty the team members were experiencing—and perhaps, partly due to their state of disequilibrium—we were able to quickly co-create a space for mutual support and discovery. Through a series of competence and capacity-building activities, team members soon began to share philosophical insights and reflect on the opportunities this change presented. They became more confident as they reaffirmed their shared human capacity to embrace rather than deny the unexpected.

I was humbled when, after years of helping organizations become more agile and innovative, I realized that the session—conducted in the very midst of the unexpected—had been one of the most rewarding and ultimately impactful I have had the honor to facilitate. In the months and years that followed that session, many of the participants did, in fact, move on to other opportunities as the company drastically downsized and reconfigured. One such participant is now a valued advisory board member at the Center I oversee at DePaul University's School for New Learning and a leader at an innovative and agile company. The enduring relationships I saw and participated in that day exemplify the power of interpersonal dynamics at the heart of this book. Something else happened in the workshop room that day, too, I realized one of the most important aspects of agility—the ability to make an *intentional* shift in order to be effective in changing contexts.

While you may not have had this particular opportunity to be agile, every person in every organization will experience the need to respond to the unexpected and unplanned in big and small ways, and will have a choice whether or not to make their own agility shift. Among the possibilities:

- Your key supplier is suddenly out of business
- Your CEO or another key leader leaves the organization
- Your phone system goes down for a few crucial hours
- A new social trend holds a significant business opportunity for the first responder
- You are asked to cut your product development cycle by 50 percent
- Your company headquarters is moving out of state or out of the country
- A new competitor enters the market
- A work stoppage takes place at your central distribution hub in Asia
- You go through a major restructuring, but you need your people to continue to collaborate effectively

Each of these examples happened to organizations I work with. While none of the organizations expected events to unfold as they did, each company was able to turn a challenge into an opportunity.

The shift from challenge to opportunity does not happen by accident, as I have seen in my years leading countless workshops with leaders, teams, and organizations that wanted to become more agile and innovative. The shift begins when one or more leaders recognizes a need and takes action (my definition of leadership in this book). Some wanted to feel more confident thinking on their feet; others needed to improve their ability to collaborate in their teams or departments while building a more responsive organizational culture. You may be surprised to learn that as I work with these organizations, in addition to the latest management research and best practices, just as often I find myself drawing on the strategies I learned in my first career as a theater director, producer, and stage manager. In regional and smaller urban nonprofit theaters I learned some of my most valuable lessons in agility—how to make optimal use of available resources, be creative under pressure, and always, always be prepared to respond to the unexpected and unplanned.

Seeing so many individuals, teams, and organizations transform as they implemented these practices led me to conduct more in-depth research. I was curious to know more about what happens for people as they are learning to improvise and be more agile. My most interesting discovery was that, rather that attribute their increased agility to new skills and knowledge, most attributed it to the context or space they co-created with their colleagues. I soon came to call this context *playspace*, and I wrote about these transformations in my book *From Workplace to Playspace*. This is not the funny hats and games kind of play, but space for:

- The *play* of new ideas
- People to *play* new roles
- More *play* in the system
- Improvised *play*

When we have the intention to create such playspace, we naturally expand our individual and collective capacity for agility. Some especially good news grew out of this research: when there is a shared intention to create playspace, it takes very little time for it to come to life. It is not dependent on long-term relationships but on the shared intention of participants to support one another's success. This is why improvisers can jump in at a moment's notice, joining a group of players with whom they have never performed, and create a delightful performance. In this case, *connecting* happens through the implicit shared experience and intention, and *building* happens in the moment on stage, as new worlds are co-created and explored.

Helping leaders, teams, and organizations create this playspace has been incredibly rewarding. However, it wasn't until I had the opportunity that I just described to support the team at the very moment they encountered life-changing unexpected news that I discovered a missing piece, one that helped bring into focus the essential dynamics of what I have come to call *the agility shift*.

Regardless of your role, you need the capacity to make the agility shift. The good news is that we all have this capacity, and we actually improvise in response to countless unplanned situations each day. The challenge is to tap into this capacity for organizational success. When a leader, team, or entire organization has this capacity, we characterize that person or group as agile. We tend to assign superhuman qualities to those who possess superior agility. In awe, we tell the tales of heroes who display agility in the direst circumstances. This book removes the mystery to reveal the mind-set, strategy, and practice shift everyday organizational heroes make and sustain for organizational success.

What's Stopping You?

Everyone agrees that there is real, tangible value in being more agile. Agile individuals are happier, healthier, and more creative and engaged; agile teams are more productive, collaborative, and innovative; and agile organizations are more profitable. In fact, there is so much value in heightened agility that many organizational leaders regularly talk about it and even write it into their strategic plans and mission statements. A McKinsey survey found that nine out of ten executives ranked agility "both as critical to business success and as growing in importance over time."[1] With all of this talk, it is surprising we don't see more organizations making significant shifts toward greater agility. This is actually the root of the problem: (1) most of the talk remains at the leadership level and (2) when there is action, it is initiated and executed using the same models and methods that inhibited agility in the first place.

To become truly agile, leaders (by whom I mean anyone who takes responsibility for responding to and discovering emerging opportunities and challenges), teams, and entire organizations need to make a fundamental shift—one that begins with a mind-set change and extends to a shift in models and methods followed at all levels of the organization.

In this book, through the stories of four very different types of organizations, you will discover the nature of this agility shift and how to make it happen for yourself, team and organization. Regardless of your role in your organization—or your position as an external consultant—this book will show you how to reach business goals by improving agile performance.

These case stories are not the stuff of corporate fairy tales, in which all of the real-life struggles and setbacks have been edited out. In fact, I chose each example to illustrate the conditions and strategies that led specific leaders, teams, and organizations to realize the urgent need to make the agility shift. All of these organizations are success stories, not because their results are pristine on any given day, news cycle, or quarterly report. They are success stories because they have made a commitment to strategies and practices that enable them to learn from each challenge, quickly find opportunities in the unexpected, and succeed over the long haul.

The Triple Bottom Line

In my years working across industries with organizations ranging from Fortune 50 companies to fifty-employee start-ups, I have been most inspired by those that measure success in terms of the "triple bottom line": people, profits, and planet. Whether they do so explicitly or implicitly, the companies I profile put people first and recognize that their success is dependent on the individual and collective strength of what I call their Relational Web. This web is a personal and system-wide network for mutual support, coordination, resources, and idea sharing. The employees who received such life- and organization-changing news just before my workshop that day, were able to be agile and effective in large part because of the strength of their Relational Web. By putting the Relational Web and the dynamic human ability to connect and build relationships and resource networks at the center of this book, I take an intentionally more humanistic approach to agility than most management experts.

In reading *The Agility Shift,* you will discover or have reaffirmed important business practices that enhance agility at every level of the system, including that of individual leaders, teams, the organization, and the entire business ecosystem. While shining a light on these aspects of the organization is not new, placing the human system at the center is a rare, and long overdue, approach. Each of the mind-set shifts, strategies, and specific practices described here are designed to sustain the health of the human system and Relational Web, which is the foundation of sustainable business results, and, ultimately, a sustainable planet.

Agility Lessons in Unfamiliar and Familiar Places

Karl Weick, one of my favorite organizational thinkers, once said, "If you want to understand organizations, study something else."[2] I have found this idea to be helpful again and again in both my own experience and in that of the organizations with which I work. Often, we can see issues and opportunities more clearly when we hear stories of leaders, teams, and organizations that are very different from our own. For this reason, don't be surprised to find yourself reading about agile airline pilots, SWAT teams, and film crews, as well as about those whose agility is highlighted in more familiar, but sometimes equally high-stakes, business settings.

I also share lessons from my own in-depth research on people who intentionally developed their agility competence, capacity, and confidence, as well as important new findings from neuroscience. Having a better awareness and understanding of how our brains and bodies are wired to respond to the unexpected and unplanned will help you be more effective when you experience VUCA and agility is paramount. Finally, while this in not a book specifically about agile methodologies, such as Scrum, originated by innovative software developers, you will learn many of their work habits and the strategies that lead to their impressive results.

You may have noticed that this book's title is a double entendre. First and foremost it references the shift all organizations must make to compete in increasingly changing contexts. But it's also about another kind of work shift. Whether you are working the night shift, the help desk shift, or the Saturday morning catching-up-on-e-mails shift, if you work for an organization that makes agility a strategic priority, you are also always working "the Agility Shift." Agility supposes that innovation, responsiveness, and performance will trump once-familiar constraints of job titles, organizational structure, and outdated processes.

Make Shift Happen

Today's best leaders are making *shift* happen. They're bravely challenging the status quo and trying unconventional methods to make real progress in the way things get done. They shake up workplace norms and show others what agility really looks like. And most importantly, they inspire their teams to follow suit. One of the most important shifts is being made in the very notion of leadership. When it comes to agility, a leader is anyone who sees an opportunity or challenge and takes responsibility for doing something about it. In this sense, anyone who is effectively making shift happen is a leader in an agile organization.

As a busy professional who is accountable for business results, I know you don't have time for lengthy conceptual and philosophical musings. I include just enough to lay a foundation in each chapter, then quickly focus on specific strategies, tactics, and methods that you can begin to implement even as you are reading, to make the shift toward a more responsive, innovative, and, yes, agile organization.

These Make Shift Happen segments invite or remind you of a mindset shift while guiding you in new strategic directions or offering specific practices. Some of these practices can be implemented the moment action is needed, while others are intended to prepare you to be effective when that moment occurs.

You Are Invited

This book was conceived and is offered as an invitation. Unlike an invitation to an event, this is an invitation to begin a process. Because this process includes a shift from the familiar and known to the unfamiliar and unknown, it may at times be uncomfortable and challenging. However, if you truly wish to become more agile and effective, you will also find the process exhilarating, renewing, and energizing. For it is when we become more comfortable being uncomfortable that we are not only most effective but are most alive.

PART ONE

Understanding the Value and Dynamics of the Agility Shift

CHAPTER ONE

The Agility Shift: What and Why

We rightly hail the heroes in history who display a remarkable capacity to be effective in the most challenging of circumstances. Captain Chesley Sullenberger had only seconds to choose a course of action after a flock of geese flew into the engines of a passenger jet he was piloting, landing safely in New York's Hudson River. The Apollo 13 astronauts had just hours to collaborate with NASA engineers on the ground to devise a way to filter the life threatening levels of CO_2 from the cabin and conserve enough power to return to earth. Sullenberger knew his disabled aircraft could not make it to a suitable runway. The Apollo 13 astronauts did not have the optimal equipment on board. Each rapidly shifted the mission, maintained an attitude of optimism, engaged and improvised with the available resources, and safely returned to earth.

> The Agility Shift is the intentional development of the competence, capacity, and confidence to learn, adapt, and innovate In changing contexts for sustainable success.

Every day, though typically in less spectacular contexts, agile leaders, teams, and organizations maintain creativity under pressure, whether in the midst of a merger, a sudden supply-chain disruption, or an unexpected business opportunity. Awareness of available resources is clearly not enough; agile organizations must have the capacity to use their resources creatively and effectively at a moment's notice in response to the unexpected. In fact, truly agile organizations have a well-developed ability to make shifts that turn those challenges into opportunities.

How do they do it? Some time ago neuroscientists discovered that, faced with extreme stress, the amygdala (located in what is sometimes referred to as the "reptilian brain" because it is thought to be the oldest in evolutionary terms), can send us into the familiar fight-or-flight response.[1] In this state, the brain is in survival mode, no longer able to fully access the prefrontal cortex, the site of executive thinking.[2] While this response is hard wired into our neural networks, agile individuals, including Captain Sullenberger, the Apollo 13 crew, and their organizations, have learned how to continue to be effective in the midst of high-stress situations. This ability does not happen by accident but through intentional and continuous development.

Think about the last time you experienced something unexpected. It could be as simple as a disruption in your morning routine or as complex and life changing as a merger, acquisition, downsizing, relocation, or other significant unplanned change. Do you remember your immediate response? Were you hijacked by your reptilian brain or were you able to be find the opportunity under stress? Perhaps you were constrained by your preconceptions about what was happening, or by your organization's culture, systems, and processes? If you were, you are not alone.

Our brains are wired to go into survival mode when we perceive a threat. It doesn't matter if this threat is to our original plan, our core beliefs, our status, or our physical survival. In the heat of the moment, the brain and the entire nervous system and body can react the same—as if our very existence is under attack. Your individual, team, and organizational success depend upon your ability to make the shift from fight, freeze, or flight to a mind-set in which you can be effective and agile.

The agility shift is dynamic, intentional, and continuous. In addition to the mind-set shift and practices presented here, this change requires that plans, agendas, and preconceptions be held lightly so that they don't eclipse new discoveries, information, and opportunities. Neither Captain Sullenberger nor the Apollo 13 crew—nor most of the employees of the company I described in the introduction—could have predicted the specific unexpected and unplanned events they encountered. However, all were able to be successful because they were prepared, or quickly became prepared, to make the necessary shifts.

These shifts originate with and are sustained by leaders, teams, and organizations that interact within human systems in the dynamic present moment. Italian organizational theorist Claudio Ciborra located the "dynamic present" somewhere between panic and boredom.[3] When we respond to the unexpected with panic or frustration, we are too paralyzed to be effective; when we respond with boredom, we are simply too disengaged to care. Somewhere in the middle, awake to the possibilities of the dynamic present moment, we develop and discover our capacity to be agile.

In the dynamic present, agile leaders, teams, and organizations are effective because they are able to quickly become aware of the current reality and reframe the challenge to reveal its opportunities. This shift is depicted in the dramatized movie account of the Apollo 13 mission when the team in the NASA control room is working feverishly to bring the astronauts home and the NASA director, after hearing a litany of the problems onboard, says, "This could be the biggest disaster NASA has ever experienced." The flight director, played by Ed Harris, turns to him and says, "With all due respect, sir, I believe this is going to be our finest hour." He then famously leads his crew with the line, "Failure is not an option."[4]

I am certainly not the first to call out these stories of creativity under pressure. I draw your attention to them precisely because they are part of our cultural lore of heroic action. It is not enough, however, to appreciate the remarkable capacity these leaders and teams, and the organizations that supported them, displayed. We must understand the nature of the thinking and actions that contributed to their success. When we do so, we can become effective as we encounter our own chaos. Though our challenges may be less dramatic and are rarely life threatening, our ability to shift from panic (or boredom) in the workplace can be the difference between disaster and triumph. The good news is that you don't need to be a seasoned pilot or have the talent of a Hollywood screenwriter to make these shifts when you encounter the disruptions, or even disasters, that are inevitable in the life of a team or organization, and certainly within the span of any career. You *do,* however, need to learn how to shift your mind-set, strategy, and day-to-day practices.

Agility Is Your Competitive Advantage

If the rapidly changing contexts you must negotiate each day are not enough to convince you of the urgent need to make agility your strategic priority, the growing body of evidence of the bottom-line benefits will surely make the case. Research conducted at the Massachusetts Institute of Technology (MIT) suggests that agile firms grow revenue 37 percent faster and generate 30 percent higher profits than non-agile companies. This same study found that an overwhelming majority of executives (88 percent) cite organizational agility as key to global success.[5] Another study on the use of agile methodologies in software development showed a 38 percent increase in productivity.[6] Additional research on learning agility, a key competency, shows that the ability to learn quickly from experience and apply the new knowledge in fresh contexts is the strongest indicator of leadership success.[7]

Captain Sullenberger displayed his learning agility on January 15, 2008. Prior to that day, in his forty-two years of flying, he had never experienced engine failure for any reason. Despite this, he maintained a mind-set that kept him from behaving as if any flight was a routine operation. Over his career as a military pilot, he had grieved the loss of twelve comrades who had perished in plane crashes. Searching for answers, Sullenberger realized that many of these pilots had not adapted to the changed reality of their situation quickly enough. Not wanting to be blamed for the loss of the multimillion dollar jets they piloted, many struggled to land, waiting past the point that they could have safely ejected and saved themselves.

This painful lesson did not go to waste. As soon as the flock of geese disabled both engines, Sullenberger was able to quickly draw on his understanding of other pilots' mistakes as well as his own years of experience. "As soon as the birds struck," he reflected, "I could have tried to return to LaGuardia so as not to ruin a US Airways aircraft. I could have worried that my decision to ditch the plane would be questioned by superiors or investigators. But I chose not to."[8] Rather than spending valuable time attempting to return the aircraft to LaGuardia, Sullenberger quickly shifted his mission to saving the lives of the 155 passengers on board by using the only viable runway available, the Hudson River.[9]

The agility shift is crucial to the survival and success of entire organizations, as it is to individuals. And the shift is even more relevant today than it was just a few short years ago—and not just because of the external, market-driven factors I cited earlier. The workforce itself is changing. I'm sure you've noticed that a new generation has arrived, and these new workers bring with them new expectations and ways of getting things done. A recent PwC study of millennials (those born in the 1980s and '90s) confirmed what most of their parents and teachers have been saying for some time: they are more attuned to working in teams, value community, and are comfortable using technology for communication and collaboration.[10] Not only are millennials particularly suited to effective action in changing conditions, they thrive in unsettled situations. Why should you care about this? Because millennials currently make up more than a third of today's workers, and by 2020 will account for almost half of an increasingly global and diverse workforce.[11] If you and your teams and organization are not making the agility shift, you are not preparing for success with those who will actually help you sustain it.

The *Real* Reason to Care About Agility

The knowledge that agile organizations are more profitable, sustainable, and innovative may be reason enough for you and your organization to make the agility shift. However, this shift is not only practical—ensuring your ability to survive and thrive—its core dynamics (interacting and interconnecting) are the key to your ability to create and experience meaning, purpose, and happiness. Yes,

I am putting meaning, purpose, and happiness at the center of the agility shift. Why? Because it is essential to fostering and sustaining the level of engagement, commitment, and creativity you need to respond effectively when the unexpected hits.

> Organizations that prioritize agility also prioritize ways of being, thinking, and acting that enable agility and create space to move, reflect, and respond effectively.

Those who are making the agility shift necessary to sustain success in a changing world are committed to mastering the strategies and processes outlined in this book. Mastery for the agility shift is unlike mastery of a specific skill; it is a continuous process and demands a commitment to developing the competence, capacity, and confidence necessary for adapting and innovating. The extrinsic rewards of increased productivity, profits, and competitiveness may be enough for you to initiate this shift; the *intrinsic* rewards of deepening purpose, meaning, and, yes, happiness will help you sustain it.

The Three Cs of the Agility Shift

So far, you have gotten a preview of the mind-set shift and state of readiness necessary for agile success. Making and sustaining this shift requires a commitment to the continuous development of the three Cs: competence, capacity, and confidence.

Agility competence consists of the skills, knowledge, and abilities necessary to respond to the unexpected and unplanned, as well as to find opportunities in new developments and emerging trends.

Agility capacity is the degree of uncertainty and volatility in which a person can be effective. For example, a team may have the competence to get a new product to market on a tight deadline, but it may not have the capacity to do so if the deadline changes several times, if the product specifications change, and/or if there is a worker strike at the manufacturing facility.

Agility confidence is the human need to trust in one's own and others' competence and capacity to be effective in changing contexts.

The Three Cs of the Agility Shift are not interchangeable, though they are interrelated. For example, without agility confidence, there is little value in agility competence and capacity; of course, any amount of agility capacity is wasted without agility competence and vice versa.

The three Cs are embedded in each of the dynamics of agility introduced in the next two chapters, as well as in the strategies and practices I outline throughout the book. Competence, of course, is only the starting point. In chapter 8, I describe specific competencies and outline how everyone, no matter his role or level of leadership, can take responsibility for developing his agility competencies and then can move beyond competence to *performance* when things don't go as planned. In fact, those who make the shift understand that "the plan" can actually be part of the problem.

From Planning to Preparing

The agility shift is also a shift from planning—with its focus on a linear process with a beginning, middle, and end resulting in an actual *plan*—to a focus on preparing, where all aspects of the system continuously develop the competence, capacity, and confidence to perform effectively in changing contexts. For those who make the agility shift, the purpose of preparing is to develop readiness for the unexpected rather than solely to execute a set plan. Captain Sullenberger took all of 208 seconds from the time the birds struck his engines to the time he landed in the Hudson. He had spent forty-two years preparing.[12]

The agility shift is not simply accelerated planning.

Lest you be tempted to cancel your annual strategic planning retreat, remember that the agility shift is not a dualistic one: either we create a plan or we prepare for the unexpected. The agility shift embraces the creative tension between planning and preparing. The act of planning serves several valuable purposes; chief among them, it helps us clarify, engage with, and recommit to our values and vision. As anyone who has participated in strategic planning, or even the plan for the office holiday party, knows that the plan itself may be the least valuable aspect and often bears little resemblance to what actually happens. Or, as the mid-nineteenth-century Prussian field marshal and war strategist Helmuth von Moltke said, "No plan survives contact with the enemy."[13] While I don't advocate relating to the unexpected and unplanned as "the enemy," simply replace those words with "current reality" and you will understand the limitations of plans.

> A plan made today is based on the assumption of a knowable future.

With a core focus shifted to preparation, or, more aptly, to *preparing* all participants to do more than adapt to change, you and your colleagues are able to leverage its opportunities for innovation.

From Events to Processes

The shift from planning to preparing is something you may have already made in another area of your life. Anyone with a gym membership knows that physical fitness is a daily commitment, a way of being in the world, not an initiative that is launched with a burst of enthusiasm, lasts a few weeks or months, and then loses steam. Agile organizations are comparable to fit individuals. Fit individuals integrate their exercise and wellness practices into their daily lives, because the outcome is not any one accomplishment but an overall quality of life and capacity to live it to its fullest. Truly fit individuals also train for more than one activity; they develop strength and flexibility in body and mind to respond to anything life throws their way. Agile organizations also maintain their strength by focusing on their core competences while regularly stretching themselves for maximum flexibility and resilience. Injured athletes and ordinary individuals recover more quickly if they are physically fit. The combination of strength and flexibility, along with the mind-set that goes with it, provides a solid foundation to rebuild a depleted system.

Physical fitness and organizational fitness are mutually reinforcing. Fitness is useful both as a metaphor and as a mind-set for agility throughout the organizational network and ecosystem, supporting faster recovery from the unexpected as well as improved capability to innovate. CEOs of major corporations such as Unilever, Whole Foods, and Apple are embracing this shift by speaking out against a shortsighted focus on quarterly returns. Marc Benioff, CEO and chairman of Salesforce, calls it simply "Wrong. The business of business isn't just about creating profits for shareholders—it's also about improving the state of the world and driving stakeholder value."[14]

Driving stakeholder value is a process, not an event. It requires organizations to make both a mind set shift and a practice shift, in which everything from preparing to learning to innovating is continuous, engaged activity rather than simply moments in time.

From Information to Interactions

We love information. Especially in times of crisis. Have you ever noticed your tendency to become glued to the television or Internet when disaster strikes? It is human nature to try to gather as much information as possible, to make sense and create meaning when we don't understand what is happening. We seek information for another reason, too: control. We operate under the illusion that if we can gain more information, we will not only understand what is happening, we might just be able to control it.

I am not suggesting that there is no value to information or to clearly defined reporting and accountability relationships for routine business operations. I am instead calling out the temptation that an information-centered approach to agility offers: there's a desire to settle into the illusion that information will give you control, when in many situations it is simply not possible to gather or process enough information to be effective when it counts.

Recognizing that there are many situations that you not only cannot control but cannot predict is a radical mind-set and practice shift for most. It requires that you decide whether your goal is to reduce the perception of uncertainty or to actually become more effective in its midst. It also involves more than a simple reconfiguration of the org chart and job descriptions. It requires relinquishing the *illusion of control* that lies at the very foundation of most management training and business practice.

This shift is being made in one of the most hierarchal, command-and-control organizations in the country, the United States military. Recognizing the insidious nature of information age strategies and their tendency to lead to either analysis paralysis or the false security of convenient stories, the U.S. military has begun to make a fundamental shift in its approach to VUCA (volatility, uncertainty, complexity, and ambiguity), a shift from *information to interactions*.[15] This change does not begin with restructuring and redeployments but with a fundamental shift in mind-set.

In fact, the term VUCA was first coined by the U.S. Army War College to describe increasingly complex and unpredictable combat conditions.[16] VUCA has become shorthand for the reality of life in the twenty-first century. Most business approaches to VUCA focus on strategies to reduce uncertainty. These strategies tend to center around gaining greater control, including amassing more and better information, minimizing risk, and improving planning and analysis.

While risk and uncertainty reduction are valid strategies, they do not necessarily make an organization more agile, for two reasons: (1) collecting more and better information takes time and may foster the illusion of control and comfort when, in reality, it is impossible to gather all available information in complex, changing contexts, let alone fully analyze and make meaning of it and (2) planning and analysis are dependent on relatively stable contexts.

Another liability of information-centered approaches is that they typically lead to more questions and the need to gather more information to reduce the uncertainty created by the information already collected. There is an even more significant liability of the information-centered approach to agility: our preconceptions lead us to filter out information that does not align with our expectations. The transcript of Sullenberger's interaction with air traffic controllers shows how quickly he shifted from information gathering to interacting with his available resources. Thirty-five seconds into the exchange, as controllers are still trying to offer alternative runways, Sullenberger replies, "We're unable. We may end up in the Hudson."[17]

Most of us will not find ourselves in literal life-or-death situations that demand an agility shift within seconds. Yet the stressful contexts we negotiate each day do include similar pitfalls. Under the stress of an unexpected challenge or opportunity, our ability to access our higher thinking capacity can be reduced, leading us to fall back on the version of the story we expected: the routine flight, the glitch-free product rollout, the seamless intercultural communication. The power of our brain's wiring and our comfort with these stories are evident in crises that did not end as well as that of US Airways Flight 1549. Warnings of terrorist threats before 9/11 and potential malfunctions of crucial components prior to the *Challenger* space shuttle disaster went unheeded because they did not fit the narrative that was co-constructed by leaders during years of experience and expectation.[18]

What stories might you and your colleagues be constructing with the information available to you? What warning signals or opportunities might you be missing in your comfort with this information? Agile leaders, teams, and organizations know they cannot afford to get caught up in a story. They are instead learning how they might be more effective by focusing on their interactions with one another *and* with the available information in the dynamic present moment.

> The mind-set shift necessary to improve agility is a change from an overreliance on information and uncertainty reduction toward intentional interaction.

Let me emphasize that this is a shift away from an *overreliance* on information. I am not suggesting you curtail important industry and market data analysis, or take this as encouragement to blindly make decisions when further investigation is warranted. I *am* encouraging you to shift away from the false comfort such information can offer, and toward the relational context in which you make sense of it, decide and act.

When we make the shift from information to interaction, we may be called to shift more than our relationship to external information; we may need to shift the way we perceive ourselves as well. The agility shift requires that we value our capacity to connect and build relationships over—or at least as much as—our hard-won expertise. Years of experience, training, and credentials are, of course, still valuable. But their value is minimal without the networks to which the skills, knowledge, experience, and resource awareness are linked. In other words, separating the process of "knowing what" and "knowing how" from the process of "knowing who" significantly diminishes agility capacity.

The shift from information to interaction values the human system in which all meaning and action take place. Rather than problematizing this system as nonobjective or messy, the agility shift embraces it and engages it more fully. You may not be able to control or predict what happens, but with a conscious, continuous commitment to interacting within your web of relationships and resources, you will be more effective than you ever imagined.

The agility shift is first and foremost a shift in mind-set. This mind-set values interactions within the dynamic present moment. It is also a shift from the false comfort of "a plan" to achieving a state of readiness to find opportunity in the unexpected. In the next chapter you will discover how to build this readiness with the most important resource you already have in your organization, your Relational Web.

CHAPTER TWO

Weaving the Relational Web for Agility

The unexpected hit Washington, Illinois, on November 17, 2013, when an EF4 tornado barreled through town, all but flattening the rural community of fifteen thousand. Thanks to weather service tornado warnings and sirens, only one resident lost his life, though hundreds were injured and many lost their homes.

Some of the most important lessons in business are learned by looking at people working together in ways that have nothing to do with generating profits. Understanding how members of these systems engage all of their available resources can inspire us to do so in our own contexts. The way people responded to the disaster shows the power of human relationships. Within minutes of the storm's passing, neighbors began calling out to one another and searching the rubble for those needing help. Almost immediately, the community as a whole recognized that they needed a better way to communicate and send help to those affected by the disaster. The Washington & Central Illinois Tornado Relief & Recovery Facebook group was quickly founded as a place for survivors to connect with resources and find their family members and friends.

People in neighboring towns soon joined the Facebook group to connect people with their lost objects and cherished family photos, some of which had blown more than a hundred miles away. Neighbors made public offers to share what they could, including lending extra vehicles to strangers who had lost their means of transportation. The way the community came together was the silver lining of a horrible tragedy.[1] "We are alive and the generosity and good wishes of everybody, our friends, family, and people we don't even know has made us so thankful," said Washington resident Kelly Stephen, who lost everything.[2] Without even knowing how or when they would need to engage it, the community had spent years preparing for this disaster by weaving a web of relationships, resources, and expertise.

The Relational Web in Action

The best way to understand the Relational Web is to reflect on your own successful encounters with the unplanned and unexpected. I will describe this web, though you already know it from your own experience. You have engaged your Relational Web when:

- You were thrown into a new and unfamiliar role or situation
- Your team was asked to quickly respond to a new opportunity and was missing expertise or key resources

- You and your organization needed to sustain your success, despite significant uncertainty and volatility

> The Relational Web is the personal and system-wide network for mutual support, coordination, and resource and idea sharing.

All human systems, whether they are families, social networks, communities, or organizations, are constructed from a web of relationships. In daily life we may be less conscious of the role this web plays in our ability to be effective. However, when we are faced with a challenge or new opportunity it is the first place most of us turn. Those who engage this web fully also tap the resources, knowledge, and experience of those within it.

Our Relational Web helps us with two essential needs in the midst of uncertainty and volatility:

- sense making (comprehending what is happening/has happened)
- meaning making (discerning and determining the significance of what is happening/has happened)

All effective action is grounded in these cycles, even if the situation demands a rapid response; sense making and meaning making are happening at both a conscious and subconscious level.

I intentionally call this set of resources a Relational *Web* because it is very much like the spiderweb that inspired it. Spun by a creature weighing fractions of an ounce, spiderwebs have a strength and resilience that are, pound for pound, ten times stronger than steel. Spiderwebs have a unique characteristic of softening and stretching (so as not to break) then stiffening (for reinforcement and protection) as needed when stressed.[3]

Beyond Social Networks

While social and other networks are aspects of your Relational Web, they are not one and the same. Unlike your social network, your Relational Web weaves through your current and past relationships with human beings, your past experiences, and your identity within various communities. This web also includes your relationships to other kinds of available resources you may draw on at a time of need (like the bits of debris and food the spider stores in her web). Your Relational Web includes:

- Active relationships with friends, colleagues, and acquaintances
- Extended and/or inactive relationships
- Skills, knowledge, and talent
- Other sources of ideas, knowledge, and expertise
- Tangible and intangible resources (such as capital, facilities, raw materials, and brand reputation)

The metaphor of the web also emphasizes the nature of the ties that connect us. Some are strong, while others are weak. Some are more relevant to our current life, and some to our past.

The nature, strength, and relevance of these relationships can also change with the context. For example, unless you were a member of the Crossroads United Methodist Church in Washington, Illinois, or a recipient of one of the three hundred holiday meals the church normally serves, you might not have considered a connection with that group to be a highly relevant relationship. However, after the tornado, with Thanksgiving only ten days away, the value in the Relational Web increased enormously as volunteers moved into action to prepare one thousand holiday meals. "We didn't lose our home, the least we can do is come and help people who have lost everything, maybe give them a little bit of holiday spirit," volunteer Deb Smith said, after finding her way to the church on Thanksgiving Day. The Relational Web is not an event but a dynamic system. Tim Hetzner of Lutheran Church Charities emphasized the importance of the community's ability to recover: "To know that people are here and are gonna be here for the long term, not just for a week. To be here in the long term, to be here for the recovery," he said.[4] Not all connections within the web are the same. Some may be stronger than others, some are primarily functional, while others include a deeper personal connection. Regardless of the current strength or type of connection, all are important to make the agility shift.

For most people, support, as well as quality of life and engagement, stems from their social bonds and networks. New (and not-so-new) research shows that agile people are connected people, and connected people are much more likely to be agile. Connected people are able to tap resources more quickly in times of crisis and opportunity. As it turns out, connected people are also happier and healthier. Studies of communities whose inhabitants lead extraordinarily long and healthy lives show that the most significant factor in their longevity is the depth of their social networks and their mutual participation in one another's lives.[5] Happiness and well-being are contagious and spread through social networks.[6] These networks give us a framework for making and preserving meaning, especially when we are confronted with the completely unexpected, and even incomprehensible, events and experiences that we encounter in the course of a lifetime.

The power of my own Relational Web was never more evident to me than during the days and months immediately following my mother's cancer diagnosis. It came at a time when each of our professional lives was in full swing in separate cities, with the expectation of many more active years to come. On short notice, I all but relocated to Louisville, Kentucky, to take care of my mom and advocate for her during her treatment. While I was not even remotely prepared for this role in my thirties (this wasn't supposed to happen for a few more decades!), it was only by engaging my own web, as well as my mother's web of friends and colleagues, that I was able to both make sense of what was happening and connect to the many resources she needed in a city that was unfamiliar to me. Her coworkers regularly brought food, provided transportation to treatments, and even came and sat with me in the hospital waiting room during an endless string of surgeries. Her friend and golf partner saved the day many times when I could not get there fast enough from my home in Chicago. In a few short months, despite all the support and a series of aggressive treatments, my mother lost her battle with cancer.

This was, of course, when I needed the support of my Relational Web more than ever. My dear friend Allison, who had lost her own mother a few years earlier, was an essential part of the web that literally held me during the days when I could not even imagine going on after such a loss. My adult students, colleagues, and other friends shared their own journeys, hope, laughter, and tears with me while my mother's web of colleagues and lifelong friends continued to be there for me, my brother, and one another as we moved through and made sense of this challenging time.

My story is far from unique. We have all had experiences that remind us of the importance and value of our Relational Web; it is with and through this web that we are able to respond, regroup, and sometimes reframe our reality to find a way forward. It's important to note that our personal and professional lives are intertwined in our web, and this only makes it stronger. It was through my Relational Web that I was able to continue to serve my clients and support my graduate students during this challenging time. By staying in relationship with all aspects of my Relational Web, I was able to tap resources and expertise that enabled me to be responsive when and where I was most needed.

The value of the Relational Web may be most familiar to us when we must respond to the unplanned, but it's equally important for identifying emerging opportunities and responding with creativity and innovation. Most new discoveries and creations aren't the work of just one person. Behind every inventor, CEO, or Nobel Prize recipient is a network of people who helped provide support and/or advice. Whether notable achievements are accomplished through professional or personal connections, they are almost always fueled by collaboration. This is just further proof of strength in the Relational Web.

The Neuroscience of the Relational Web

We are hard wired to weave a Relational Web. Without the ability to connect with others and maintain relationships, humans cannot survive. Neuroscientist and psychotherapist Louis Cozolino has spent years studying the neuroscience of relationships. He, along with others in the field, confirm the neurobiological effects of what social scientists have been telling us for years: our brain depends on mutually stimulating and beneficial interactions with others for its very survival, and without such interaction "people and neurons wither and die."[7] Human physiology has evolved to support our ability to maintain the relationships that are core to our survival. In fact, the neocortex—the area of the brain where we process social stimuli, attune to and empathize with others, and identify facial expressions—is more complex in humans than in any other mammal.

Other aspects of human physiology have also evolved in a way that allows us to quickly read and process others' emotional states and demeanor. For example, in most mammals the iris and surrounding eye tissue (sclera) are the same color, making it difficult to identify the focus of another's gaze. This is a helpful characteristic for predators and prey alike. In humans, the sclera is white, better revealing the focus of our gaze, which is important for interpersonal communication, relationship building, and intimacy. While humans still have a robust fight, freeze, or flight capacity encoded in our brain structure, there is a clear evolutionary shift toward connecting and building relationships with others. Human faces express emotions and internal states often before we are even aware of them ourselves, sometimes making it impossible not to share our emotions with others.[8]

Of course, we first determine whether or not those other humans pose a threat to our survival. You may not even be aware that, on some level, your brain is assessing for threat as you walk down the street, ride the subway, or have other encounters. In organizational contexts this assessment may be more attuned to the emotional risks of social relationships, such as risks to image, credibility, and status. No one wants to look incompetent in front of her boss or colleagues or make a fool of herself during a big presentation. When we perceive such threats, our brain becomes concerned with our survival because, unfortunately, it does not always distinguish between physical and social threats. When this happens we have less access to those regions of the brain where complex and creative thinking happen. This is why, sometimes when we most need to be able to think on our feet, the perfect response or action eludes us. Just as we are less likely to crack jokes, which requires access to complex thinking, and a certain sense of safety, when we are threatened, we are also less likely to behave in ways that can expand our Relational Web when we are in protection mode.

> The brain's hard wired response to social/emotional threat is why it is so important to co-create a context that is safe enough for people to take risks and experiment.[9]

A safe context is especially important in any context where we want to set people up for innovation and learning success. Many of the practices described throughout this book will help you create an environment of safety. You will also discover strategies to ensure your organization balances this support with the challenge and provocation, so necessary for innovation and learning.

Once we have established, sometimes in a nanosecond, that we are safe enough in our social environment we begin to build those all-important connections. And, as these connections grow and deepen, our confidence in them also grows.

A robust Relational Web has additional value. Research has shown a clear link between an individual's social network and his ability to cope with stress. Steven Southwick and Dennis Charney conducted a study that showed that higher levels of oxytocin (the hormone that moderates the stress hormone cortisol) are released during social interaction. With reduced stress, individuals experience lower engagement of the amygdala (the primal region of the brain) and a greater access to the prefrontal cortex, where executive thinking takes place.[10]

To understand how these hormones behave, think about how you might feel if you were lost in an unfamiliar place by yourself. Now think about how you would feel if you were in the same situation but had a friend with you. While being lost might induce some degree of stress, you're likely to feel better when you aren't alone. The social network appears not only to help reduce anxiety in the midst of uncertainty but to improve effectiveness as well.[11] In other words, with a travel companion, you might find your way quicker than you would on your own because your brain can think more clearly.

Our membership in a social network can also enhance our creativity. New research shows that identifying oneself with a group that is perceived to be creative enhances both the degree of individual creativity and the likelihood of group creativity.[12] Positive associations with a social network are developed over time through interacting, learning, and cocreating. A growing body of research reinforces the need to attune and attend to the health of our interpersonal relationships within the Relational Web to enhance agility.

The Brain is Wired to Be Social for Our Own Survival

While no one could have predicted the tornado that hit Washington, Illinois, the community was prepared when it struck. People of the town had woven a Relational Web that enabled them to engage one another and all of their available resources during a devastating time. Less than a week after the tornado hit, the local high school's undefeated football team was scheduled to play in the semifinals. Ten of the team's players had lost their homes, while others' homes had significant damage. The coach cancelled practice the first few days after the tornado, instead volunteering his team to help their neighbors sort through the wreckage and recover items of meaning or value. At first, it was unclear whether or not the big game would be played at all.

Everyone was functioning day to day, and only by engaging with their individual and intertwined Relational Web did community members begin to find a way forward. In the midst of extreme disruption, the team and the entire community drew on their social, technological, and ecosystem networks and discovered a capacity well beyond that of their immediate classmates, family, friends, and community.

The decision was made to go ahead with the game, despite the devastation to the area. The community needed to come together, and this was a chance to focus on something other than their loss and grief, if only for a few hours. The opposing team, the Springfield Sacred Heart Cyclones, was keenly aware of the chaos their rivals were experiencing. They sent several charter buses to Washington so family and community members could attend the game in Springfield. Upon their arrival, team and community members were greeted with a welcome banner reading "God Bless Washington" hanging over the Cyclone bleachers. While the Panthers did not win the game, they did win the hearts of all who attended, and the game gave a needed boost to the players, coaching staff, and community.[13]

When the Relational Web is intentionally engaged, as it is in times of personal challenge or disaster, or in response to unexpected opportunities, it expands and strengthens just like a spider's web. With each new connection, more people and resources are invited in. Each new person brings her networks and resources, creating even more capacity and opportunity. I have invited you to renew your awareness and appreciation of your own Relational Web through examples and stories from our shared human experience. As you will soon see, this shared experience and the connections we weave are essential to the agility shift dynamics in organizations.

CHAPTER THREE

Discovering the Five Dynamics
of the Agility Shift

The most effective and agile leaders, teams, and organizations do more than weave a strong Relational Web. They adopt a mindset, strategy, and practices that ensure they are relevant, responsive, resilient, resourceful, and reflective. I first identified these five dynamics when I conducted my own research, but also noted the dynamics showing up in other important research on agile leaders, teams, and organizations. These same dynamics became evident in my work with businesses across industries, from Fortune 50 companies to those with fewer than fifty employees.

You likely will recognize some of these five dynamics from business best practices. For example, the concept that organizations must be responsive and resilient to thrive in today's world isn't a novel one. It is new, however, to implement a strategy that weaves a Relational Web into each of these practices to build a sustainably agile system.

I came to call these agility shift *dynamics* because they are just that: dynamic qualities and characteristics that come to life through consistent, intentional practice. Each of these dynamics represents a distinct dimension of agility that my clients and many other organizations practice to achieve sustained success. After a brief description of each dynamic, I share the "Make Shift Happen" practices that will help strengthen that dynamic in your own organization. The case

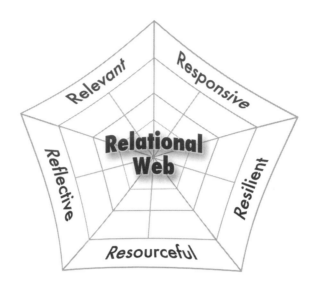

stories that conclude each dynamic show how an organization first bumped up against its need to make the agility shift, and then discusses how each developed its competence, capacity, and confidence to renew itself and deliver business results.

Agile Organizations Are Relevant

Simon Sinek makes a strong case for relevance as the foundation for action in his popular TED talk and book *Start with Why*.[1] Many individuals and organizations make the mistake of focusing on the "what" or "how" without grounding it in a "why." (As in, "*why* is this relevant?") In this relational dynamic, relevance is the awareness, understanding, and alignment of values and purpose with the overall success of the organization. Without a "why"—a clear sense of purpose—we are easily distracted and confused by the noise all around us.

> Relevant organizations use their "why?" to guide their "how?"

One sign of organizations that are guided by their purpose is their tendency to empower employees. While these companies focus on outcomes as indicators of success, their people are free to make decisions about the way those outcomes are achieved. Without micromanagement, both people and companies are more effective, innovative, and, yes, agile. Agile leaders, teams, and organizations make the shift from how to why.

The sense of purpose that drives relevance is a critical success factor for making the agility shift and realizing results. Agile individuals and organizations are relevant first to their own values and second to the needs of their customers; they actively use this relevance to guide all their endeavors. Members of agile organizations possess the ability to scan the environment for information and emerging trends, and then they filter and assess that information so they can respond effectively. It is impossible to scan, assess, decide, and act without knowing what information, trends, and patterns are relevant to your purpose and passion. Of course, it is also impossible to know what is relevant without a lively and passionate awareness *of* and commitment *to* your individual and organizational purpose.

It is much easier to distinguish between significant and insignificant developments and information when we are aware of our values and purpose. Clarity of purpose helps us determine whether to seize a new job opportunity, take that "stretch assignment," or begin an entirely new venture. This clarity also allows us, in the moment, to distinguish something that needs immediate attention from a new development that can be monitored over time. Of course, the time to be sure we have this awareness and confidence in our convictions is not when we are in the midst of a challenge or opportunity. This may be the time to affirm those convictions, but it's not a good time to begin the process of assessment.

At first, promoting relevance in the workplace may seem like one more thing to think about, until you realize the bottom-line benefits. People are more likely to be engaged when they know their work is relevant and has purpose, and that they are making a difference. Engaged employees persevere in the face of obstacles, and are more likely to take initiative, innovate, and be responsive to emerging opportunities.[2] Without relevance, there is little chance of engagement, and without engagement there is virtually no chance of agility.

Mightybytes, Inc.: The Agility Shift Begins with Relevance

While it's important to consider the "why" behind daily tasks and projects, focusing on the big-picture "why" can have a much larger impact, dramatically changing an organization's direction. Digital media firm Mightybytes, Inc., was reincarnated when its founder, Tim Frick, had a crisis of conscience. Although the business was doing well and Frick had more website design work than he could handle, he suddenly realized he was no longer doing what he wanted to do. "In the late '90s you couldn't swing a cat without hitting a bag of Internet money," said Frick. As many business owners do, he responded to the market and capitalized on the opportunity by rapidly expanding his team. They spent several years working at a breakneck pace, with minimal work–life balance.

One day, in the midst of working on a large new project for a national fast food chain, sleepless and suffering from full-blown bronchitis, Frick had an epiphany. "This is not the life I want," he recalls thinking. "This work doesn't have anything to do with what I care about, or what difference I want to make in the world." This realization was a major turning point for Frick, and led to a rebirth of his company. His team refocused on doing work with meaning and branding their company as one that helps businesses that want to increase sustainability, both their own and the environment's.

For Frick, the focus on relevance now starts during the hiring process. "We take the time to hire people who understand and value being a conscious company. This means they are already thinking about the planet, sustainability, and social justice. When it comes time to make decisions in the midst of a project (or even whether or not to take on a new project) we are able to quickly act based on our shared values." Today, Mightybytes consistently attracts and retains talent that shares its triple-bottom-line values of people, planet, and profits. Not only did Mightybytes change to align with what's relevant to Frick, it has expanded organically and increased its revenue 87 percent.

In 2012, Mightybytes adopted a new approach to its work, with relevance in mind. Rather than focusing on fixed outcomes for clients, the Mightybytes team embraced a dynamic, iterative process. This shift means the development team and client keep a constant eye on progress and adjust as new discoveries are made. This attitude of inquiry has led to the development of several innovative new products and client solutions, and has become a core part of the company's brand.[3]

Alignment is one of those management and organizational development terms that is so overused it has lost its power and urgency in most organizations. Just as the shift from networks to networking restores the opportunity for cocreating in the dynamic present, so does a shift from the static "alignment" to the more dynamic "aligning." The commitment to integrating core beliefs, values, and purpose with daily decision making and action is not a onetime event, accomplished at the annual strategic planning retreat.

In fact, agile organizations don't think of the strategic plan as the end product of strategic planning. The plan itself is simply the by-product of continuous preparation and capacity development.

Regular reflection on values and purpose/mission builds the capacity and conviction necessary to decide whether to jump on a new product or service opportunity, or to join a potentially lucrative new collaboration or strategic alliance. The Make Shift Happen practices that follow will help you increase relevancy throughout your organization.

Make Shift Happen

Give Everyone a Chance to SOAR

Make opportunities for everyone in your organization to discover how their values and strengths align with those of the organization.

Mightybytes is just one of my client organizations that initiated and/or sustains its agility shift by conducting regular SOAR sessions. Developed as an alternative to more traditional SWOT (strengths, weaknesses, opportunities, and threats) analyses, SOAR stands for strengths, opportunities, aspirations, and results. While SWOT leads people to focus mainly on what is not working and to strategize in reaction to the competition, SOAR harnesses organizational strengths, passions, and values to fuel innovation and engagement.[4]

At Mightybytes, these sessions have been affirming of the company's core values while making room for surprising discoveries and insights. One year, in the midst of a SOAR session I was leading for the company, I asked employees what they were most passionate about. Their unanimous answer was "brewing beer!" This recreational activity had begun in the Mightybytes kitchen on occasional Friday afternoons and had become a favorite social activity and opportunity for informal learning and connecting. After the SOAR session realization, the company made beer brewing a regular part of new team member orientation and often gives the gift of beer to its clients to celebrate a successful project launch. Subsequent SOAR sessions have led to community engagement projects, company involvement in the B Corp sustainable-business movement, and the development of innovative new products such as the Ecograder website sustainability tool, which scans websites and provides suggestions for how they could be more sustainable, by using less energy. Mightybytes is now a leader in sustainable web design. Whether or not you adopt the SOAR practice, creating regular opportunities to reengage with your strengths and passions will keep you connected to your "why?" and spur the engagement and enthusiasm at the center of your agility shift.

Agile Organizations Are Responsive

Responsive organizations have the ability to respond quickly and effectively to the unexpected and unplanned, as well as to emerging opportunities.

If you have ever said or done something you later regretted, you likely know the difference between being responsive and being reactive. Reactive behavior is likely to come from a habitual response triggered by fear or a need to control or protect. Reactive behavior is rarely effective. Responsive action is different; it may take place in the same amount of clock time that reactive action does, but it is done in the dynamic present, with full access to available resources and options. Responsive individuals and entities are able to recognize and capitalize on emerging opportunities and draw on these resources, including their intuition, while staying grounded in the present moment. Responsive individuals, organizations, and networks are response-*able*. Without the ability to respond, there is, of course, no agility.

Responsive action has the integrity of values and beliefs and is more likely to be aligned with your core purpose than reactive action. Agile leaders, teams, and organizations intentionally make shifts that enable them to be responsive rather than reactive. Responsiveness is embedded in organizational cultures that hire responsive individuals and then reinforce, recognize, and reward this behavior. Engaged employees consistently respond in the moment to an opportunity or issue not because it says so in their employee handbook or because they were taught to do so in a training session, but because they care enough to exert the discretionary effort. They also do so because they know they work in a culture that values and recognizes responsive action.

Responsive action is effective action. Of course, everyone wants to be more effective, but few people consistently attend to the key dimensions of effectiveness that link to agility. David Alberts, former American director of research for the Office of the Assistant Secretary of Defense (OASD) was instrumental in helping the military shift its mind-set and strategy to become more effective in VUCA. According to Alberts, an effective response: (1) resolves the situation and/or; (2) positively responds to the opportunity; and, (3) makes optimal use of available resources.[5] A truly effective response also expands the capacity of the individuals and entities involved. Agile leaders, teams, and organizations are aware of their level of effectiveness and consistently identify what worked and what could have been done differently. With each action-reflection cycle they improve their ability to respond effectively in the moment.

Make Shift Happen

Track Your Timeliness

Use both relative and actual timeliness as an indicator of responsiveness.

Responsiveness is measured both by the quality of action and the clock time it takes to respond, as well as by the time it takes *relative to the actual challenge or opportunity*.[6] Two days might be an eternity in response to a pressing customer need, while five months may be a lightning-fast time frame to take a product to market in response to a new opportunity. Timeliness trumps perfection every time. Customers and new opportunities alike will not wait for the perfect solution; they demand a timely response. Make sure you and your team regularly assess and track your success in being responsive from both a quality and a timeliness standpoint. Add actual and relative timeliness to your indicators of responsiveness success. As you assess your effectiveness in each category, pay particular attention to the things you and your colleagues did and the systems and processes that enabled responsiveness for insights on how you can be more intentional.

Give and Take Decision Rights and Processes

Empower employees at all levels to respond immediately to issues within their span of control to serve their customers and/or the needs of the business. If you're an employee who hasn't been given these rights, you may just need to take them.

In an MIT study of agility, 61 percent of respondents identified rapid decision making and execution as defining attributes of an agile business.[7] You know the importance of effective and timely decision rights and processes if you have ever become aware of an urgent need or compelling opportunity and brought it to the attention of the appropriate leader, only to see it languish on her desk or, worse, be given to a committee. Agile individuals and entities are able to be effective because they do not lose precious time and momentum in the morass of complex decision-making processes or leadership voids.

Umpqua Bank: Empowering Responsiveness

When Ray Davis took over as CEO of a small community bank based in Portland, Oregon, he made a commitment to create a different kind of financial institution, one that made customer and employee engagement its first priority. Since 1994, Davis and his team have grown Umpqua Bank from six locations to almost four hundred and have increased the company's total assets from $140 million to $22 billion. Umpqua sustained its growth through the banking crisis and recession, largely through its unwavering commitment to customer responsiveness and by avoiding the short-term gains made through subprime mortgages.

One of the central methods Umpqua uses to ensure responsiveness is its training strategy; all frontline personnel are cross-trained as "universal associates" and empowered to respond to customer needs in the moment. Davis walks the walk himself, and has had a red hotline phone that's connected to the phone on his desk installed in the lobby of every Umpqua location. Any customer who has an issue, question, or comment is invited to pick up the phone and call the CEO directly. If Davis is in his office, he will answer the phone himself; if he is in a meeting, he will call you right back.

Bankers know it is hard to compete solely on products and prices. The difference between interest rates and offerings from one bank to another is often negligible. That's why Umpqua competes in the space where it knows it can truly stand out, by responding to customers with what they need when they need it.[8]

This level of customer service is a high bar to reach, but when you do, you might hear your customers describe mundane tasks like depositing checks as "the highlight of my day," which is how a recent Umpqua customer characterized her visit to the bank.[9]

Davis's approach to responsiveness has fostered this value as a priority in Umpqua's culture across the company. Portland experienced a rare blizzard a few years ago that all but shut down the city.

Umpqua Bank and a lone Starbucks had been the first businesses to locate stores in a redeveloping area of the downtown, and the morning after the storm nothing was open in the developing area, not even the Starbucks. Umpqua branch manager Kay Levis decided the pioneering residents would appreciate a place to gather. While she could have stayed cozy in her own home, enjoying a snow day, Levis decided to open her store location, brew some Umpqua blend coffee, and put out some pastries. Before long, the store was filled with neighbors happy for a place to connect, share their stories, and get warm. No one remembers how much banking got done that day; everyone remembers the way the bank responded.[10]

Whether you are responding to a single unexpected event or to a large-scale opportunity, when you are present in the moment with embodied awareness, you gain valuable insight that allows you to take action much more quickly and effectively than your competitors. What's more, you're likely to become an inspiration to others and help them increase their capacity to be agile.

Agile Organizations Are Resilient

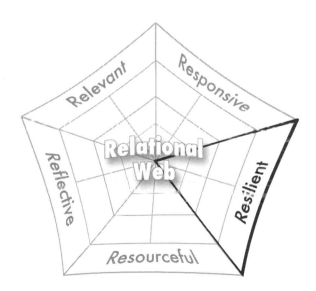

> Resilient organizations regroup, reorganize, and renew in response
> to a significant disruption.

Resilience is a tricky dynamic to assess when everything is going smoothly. How do you know if you or your organization will bounce back efficiently if you aren't put to the test? We describe certain materials and natural systems, such as rubber bands and forests, as resilient if they return to their original state relatively quickly after being stretched or damaged. Human beings are resilient when we find our way back to some level of normalcy after significant loss or other upheaval. Researchers have also identified qualities such as hardiness and grit that enable adults to persevere through difficult changes and challenges.[11] These characteristics separate those who abandon ship (and hope) at the first sign of disruption from those who harness their Relational Web and core values and find their way to innovative solutions.

In the midst of VUCA (volatility, uncertainty, complexity, and ambiguity), resilience may not be about returning to normalcy, or business as usual, as much as it is about transforming and adapting to altogether new forms, states, and routines. Given the nature of resilience, people must often adapt to circumstances that are not only unplanned but deeply undesirable.

Accounts of those who have survived conditions more extreme than most of us could ever imagine, including POWs, Holocaust survivors, and kidnapping victims, reveal that one of the most important factors in their survival was their ability to imagine and create a life beyond their trauma. In other words, they held onto an attitude of optimism.[12] Even in their darkest moments, survivors report that they found a reason to endure and hope for a positive outcome. Thriving in change and uncertainty does not mean putting on rose-colored-glasses, but instead embracing what researchers Karen Reivich and Andrew Shatté term "realistic optimism," optimism that includes the current reality.[13] With a realistic understanding of the circumstances, resilient people shift to a positive relationship to the givens of the situation to inspire a constructive attitude and action.

After a reality check about what true resilience means, fostering it in the workplace seems significantly more manageable. A variety of circumstances require resilience: supply chain disruptions, brand crises, natural disasters, geopolitical unrest, consumer demand, abrupt changes in leadership, mergers and acquisitions, product defects, and even scandal. While foreseeing these challenges can be difficult, being ready for them is within an organization's span of control. To make sure you're poised and ready to bounce back (or forward) from these situations, consider implementing the following Make Shift Happen practices in your organization.

Make Shift Happen

Designate Understudies

Identify the key roles and systems that, if they were unexpectedly unavailable, would make it impossible for your "show" to go on. With this list in hand, cross-train understudies for each of these mission-critical roles and find backup systems for your most critical infrastructure.

In recent years, just-in-time supply chain practices and lean principles have permeated manufacturing and other industries. The focus on value and efficiency is admirable; however, leaders must be cautious that their organizations are not so lean that they lose capacity to be agile in response to the unexpected. Every system that must persevere, even (and especially) if one or more aspect is disabled, should be designed for redundancy. Just like long-running plays have understudies for every role, large manufacturers should have multiple supply chain options.

Ask "What If?" and Play with Scenarios

Generate a list of unlikely but potentially disastrous events or situations for your organization and imagine how you would engage the people and resources within your Relational Web to respond. Conduct the same exercise with unlikely but highly positive opportunities to expand your capacity for resilience.

Fostering individual and organizational flexibility is less costly and has more day-to-day benefits than creating redundancy in the system. Organizations may assess the cost of creating redundancy in some systems and choose a complementary strategy of flexibility. By routinely discussing possible scenarios, you will become more comfortable facing unexpected developments.

Take a page from those who regularly train for unpredictable high-stakes situations. Ideally, weave various disaster/opportunity scenario play into your training or off-site time to give your people the chance to think on their feet in a simulated situation. If this is not feasible, talk through these imagined scenarios with your team and regularly ask "what if..." questions to provoke nonroutine thinking.

Ericsson: Resilience in Action

Swedish telecommunications company Ericsson is an excellent example of an organization that wasn't initially resilient, but which learned resilience after some important lessons in agility. In 2000, a small fire caused by a power surge in the electrical grid destroyed a crucial supply of chips at a supplier's plant in Albuquerque, New Mexico. Ericsson leaders, upon hearing of the fire, chose to trust the information they were getting from the supplier, which initially signaled that the plant would be up and running again within a week. A spokesperson for Ericsson at the time reflected, "The fire was not perceived to be a major catastrophe."[14]

Nokia, which depended on that same supplier as its main source for cell phone chips, responded very differently. Within hours of receiving the news of the fire, it mobilized an international team of supply engineers, chip designers, and top managers. Nokia's awareness of the serious nature of the problem and its ability to tap its Relational Web of experts to find alternative sources for the crucial component enabled it to respond to the crisis effectively. Reflecting on the event, Pertti Korhonen, who was troubleshooting for Nokia, said, "We didn't go into denial...a crisis is the moment you improvise."[15]

Less than a year after the event, Nokia's market share was up 3 percent, while Ericsson's was down 3 percent, and the company assigned $400 million in lost revenue to the supply chain disruption. In 2011, Ericsson sold the remaining shares of Sony Ericsson to Sony, getting out of the mobile phone business entirely. Though it was not resilient at the time, Ericsson learned valuable lessons from what is now widely referred to as "the Albuquerque Accident." Jan Wäreby, who oversaw the mobile phone division at the time, said, "We will never be exposed like that again."[16]

Today, Ericsson's telecommunications network service business is thriving because of a renewed focus on agility. Contingency planning at Ericsson now consists of three comprehensive steps, the response plan, the recovery plan, and the restoration plan, as well as a robust SCRM (supply chain risk management) strategy.[17] The company's tagline at the time of the disaster was "Make Yourself Heard," but today it's "Fast, Flexible, and In Control: Meet the Agile Operator."

Like Ericsson, many organizations with the capacity to bounce forward from a significant disruption have not become resilient by chance. They recognized that if they were to survive and thrive, they must make the agility shift a strategic priority that is reinforced and sustained throughout the organizational system. The agility shift allows companies to be resilient when it matters most. Even more than a shift in taglines or operations, it is a shift in mind-set. Today, Ericsson embraces the philosophy that "everyone is a risk manager."[18]

Agile Organizations Are Resourceful

> Resourceful organizations are aware of, use, and improvise with all available resources—human, technical, and environmental.

Resourcefulness does not mean being full of resources. It's the ability to use and improvise with the resources you do have, while being aware of what you don't have. The ability to be resourceful differentiates those who simply react to turbulence from those who use it as a provocation for creativity and innovation under pressure.

A key part of being resourceful is learning to "play within the givens." Sometimes people think more options makes everything easier, but in fact, unlimited resources can distract us from the key opportunity or problem and, paradoxically, stifle creativity. With abundant resources, significant time is spent accumulating more resources and exploring the multiple courses of action possible with those resources. Breakthroughs and new directions in the arts, sciences, and technology, as well as social innovations, are more likely to happen at the intersection of need, opportunity, and available resources than when an individual or company spends time waiting or searching for optimal resources.

A great example of playing with the givens comes from improvisational theater. Some of the most delightful evenings for audiences and actors alike are inspired by a single suggestion. Actors often invite the audience to set the scene or choose a character, and the actors deftly take it from there—without costumes or props.

The core principle of improvisation is to say, "Yes, and…" while supporting the scene with further detail. Successful improvisers accept whatever they are given, no matter how outlandish, and build on that scenario with delight and curiosity. They are resourceful because they work quickly with limited options rather than lamenting that they are stuck in a narrowly defined scene. If the audience says the players are scuba diving, the actors don't moan and groan about not having enough to work with. They immediately start making more discoveries: one player dives into a sea of Jell-O, another adds the squishing sound, another fights off the dangerous gummy sharks while grumbling about the reason they're traveling in the first place—to search for the lost magic hub cap. Specific scenes always seem funnier than broad suggestions, such as being at a park or riding in the car, because the givens are easier for the players to accept and build upon. Improvisers' ability to innovate and respond to the unexpected is not hindered by limited resources. In fact, the constraints actually help unleash the actors' creativity!

In the workplace, we have an even wider array of resources to tap than actors do in the theater. We're also "on stage" for much longer—some would say our whole careers. What can we do in this time to cultivate resourcefulness? First and foremost, we shouldn't wait for a challenging "scene" to be presented. Agile organizations are always preparing to draw on their available resources, starting with the lively networks and active networking within their Relational Web. This important resource is a built-in support system we can turn to anytime, not just when we encounter the unexpected. In addition to our people web, we should stay aware of the resources and givens in our environment so we can recognize options to support agility and innovation. Environmental factors include anything from familiar or new technology to industry news to advances by other companies. As the following case study shows, resourcefulness is an intentional process, and one that makes a significant difference in a company's success.

UPS: Making Optimal Use of Available Resources

Founded in 1907 in the basement of a saloon, UPS is now the world's largest package delivery company. Headquartered in Atlanta, the company delivers sixteen million packages a day (and up to twenty-nine million during the Christmas holiday season) in 220 countries and territories. UPS's founding story and sustained growth offer worthy inspiration for both entrepreneurs and global companies; its ability to be resourceful in response to the unexpected, as well as to new opportunities, makes it deserving of deeper study.

UPS leaders know that they have to be able to count on their 400,000 employees to work together to get packages to their destination each day. UPS taps its human resources, learning and development, and communications functions to create a culture of employee engagement. This "ownership culture" translates into intrinsic motivation for employees to be responsive and resourceful under pressure. The "whatever it takes" philosophy at UPS and its attitude of resourcefulness have saved the day numerous times when others were stopped in their tracks.

For UPS, the "whatever it takes" philosophy translates to both a strategy and a mind-set for resourcefulness at all levels of the organization. During the most predictable peak time—spanning the period just before the U.S. Thanksgiving holiday and extending until after Christmas—vacation time and personal days are suspended. In addition, to ensure that managers across the system are available, managers are taken off major projects that might keep them from being able to drop what they are doing and respond. Lee Weir, now serving as UPS's Global Leadership College facilitator, is one of the many managers who has worked his way up from entry-level jobs in the organization. He said that when the call goes out for resources, "You do the role that's necessary to get the job done as a group and as a team. My phone could ring at any time and I could get the message, 'Hey, we need you here.'" Weir, like other managers, anticipates these calls, and this preparedness allows UPS to quickly utilize employees as resources throughout the country.

UPS has a long history of using available resources to respond to the unexpected, including weather events and natural and human disasters. During the 2004 Canadian work stoppage, the company's established sorting stations, with their automated conveyor belts, were not available, but within hours leaders set up a makeshift sorting station in the parking lot of a Toronto golf course. Weir recalls, "We just backed in all these trailers that had the packages in them. We brought the brown package carriers that you see on the street, did a mini sort at four in the morning until six in the morning on that Tuesday. We delivered Tuesday and Wednesday, and all the partners that were from the States had a return flight Wednesday night to get home for Thanksgiving."[19]

The difference between organizations that are realizing results and those that are not is that agile organizations not only respond to crisis, they turn it into opportunity: opportunity for reflection, learning, and expanded capacity. In the winter of 2013, UPS experienced a perfect storm: a literal storm that swept across the country, canceling flights, creating treacherous driving conditions, and downing power lines. This, together with a 10 percent increase in online shopping that was beyond all predictions, flooded the system with packages in the crucial delivery days before Christmas. Recognizing the need and opportunity to expand their capacity for agility, David Abney, COO of UPS, in early 2014 convened a think tank of business unit leaders across the company to conduct an inquiry and solution-finding process. Additionally, Abney sent a survey to line workers, drivers, and others who work with the parcels moving through the system each day. He wanted feedback from all levels of employees on what UPS could change to make things run more smoothly. Abney received hundreds of suggestions.

Within weeks, the company announced it would make a $500 million investment to expand its capacity and upgrade its tracking system, as well as improve collaboration with retailers to better prepare for the holiday volume.[20] The results were impressive: in 2014 UPS boasted 98 percent on-time delivery (a 15 percent increase from the previous year).[21]

This degree of whole-system resourcefulness will be increasingly important in the coming years, as UPS anticipates double the volume in packages in its system by 2017. This strategy is having a positive impact on the company's brand identity. In February 2015, UPS rose to number forty-four on Forbes list of most valuable brands.[22] You don't need to be a global organization to expand your resourcefulness capacity. The Make Shift practices below can be adopted by organizations of all sizes to enhance agility.

Make Shift Happen

Leave Room in Your Truck

Make it a regular practice to check your own and your collaborators' work and cognitive load.

If the unexpected happened, could you access the resources you need to respond effectively? Do you have room to respond to new opportunities and experiment with new ideas? UPS takes the concept of giving employees room for resourcefulness very seriously. In fact, making this room starts in the delivery trucks. Weir likens the challenge of delivering packages during peak times to trying to stuff fifteen pounds of potatoes into a ten-pound bag: "What do you do? One thought is you just cram it in there with a shoehorn. Now the driver has no room to be able to process [packages]. And when you look at the door and you see the truck packed top to bottom, front to back, that can be fairly demoralizing at the start of the day." Rather than cram all eight available sections of the truck, Weir explains, they leave the last two sections at the warehouse to pack later in the afternoon. "[This way] it doesn't look overwhelming, from the viewpoint of the driver when they come in in the morning," Weir explained. "Drivers realize they have a fighting chance."[23]

If your metaphorical delivery truck is so full that you cannot even turn around in it, your ability to be agile is compromised. If the unexpected happened, could you effectively access the resources to respond? Do you have room to respond to new opportunities and experiment with new ideas?

Practice Bricolage

Build your capacity by playing with your available resources for both innovation and problem solving.

"Bricolage" describes the capacity to create with available resources. To be agile, a bricoleur must not only be aware of available resources, she must be confident in her ability to improvise with them. To build agility, find creative ways to expand resource awareness and practice bricolage;

one example is the regular "Lunch 'n' Learn" sessions presented by Mightybytes employees. Or you might share case studies of unexpected opportunities and brainstorm how you would tap your resources and relational core to respond. Better yet, follow Mightybytes's lead and unite two seemingly unrelated activities to leverage creativity, as did Mightybytes by combining employees' love of brewing with their passion for brainstorming in regular "brewstorming" sessions!

All of the organizations profiled in this book have intentionally made room, physically, mentally, and logistically, to draw on their available resources. Rather than filling their literal and metaphorical delivery truck to capacity, they leave space for movement. Resourcefulness, then, is not dependent on the number of resources available, but on your capacity to pay attention to what is happening and to tap available resources within your Relational Web in the moment.

Agile Organizations Are Reflective

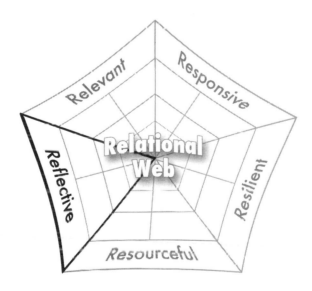

Reflective organizations learn from experience.

None of the agility shift dynamics described so far are possible without the last all-important dynamic of reflection. Through reflection you determine which new developments and opportunities are Relevant to your organization, when responsiveness is warranted. How else, but with reflection, could you evaluate your success and understand opportunities for improvement? Reflection can happen in the moment, as well as when we intentionally set time aside. All of the companies profiled in this book make this essential dynamic a regular part of their business:

• A small group of developers at Mightybytes huddles to discuss the project's progress and to test the latest iteration of the application, while the entire company holds regular SOAR sessions, described earlier in this chapter.

• A UPS driver receives real-time information on his mobile device, as well as one-on-one coaching during a ride-along with his immediate on-road supervisor; they both look forward to their morning three-minute PCM (prework communication meeting) for the latest safety tips and news.

• Scrum masters trained at Ericsson's Center for Excellence ask what impediments the company encountered in the last innovation cycle, and immediately get to work removing them.

• A universal associate at Umpqua Bank saves the day by delivering crucial documents (and a hot meal) when she learns her customer's husband is seriously ill and cannot come into the bank to sign papers; all Umpqua employees across almost four hundred locations gather at the start of each day for a "Motivational Moment" to get energized and build the relational knowledge necessary to sustain agility.

Each of the examples above illustrates ways that leaders, teams, and organizations in very different industries and settings make the agility shift each day, and even each moment, by expanding their capacity for reflection. Being reflective may sound simple enough, but it's often the last thing on people's minds, especially in unexpected or unfamiliar situations. Sometimes responding is hard enough that we don't take the time to learn the lessons and new skills that are presenting themselves to us. However, time is not the biggest obstacle to reflection; once again, the largest stumbling block is our mind-set. When we shift our mind-set to prioritize agility, we also prioritize both reflecting-in-action, as well as making the time to reflect-on-action.

First and foremost, we have to be intentional, continuously asking ourselves:

- What is happening (or has happened)?
- What new information/guidance can we draw from our experience?
- How can we incorporate this new information/guidance into our attitudes, beliefs, and actions going forward?

If we ask these types of questions proactively, the chances of learning are far greater; rather than thinking of reflection and learning as separate from action, it is *part* of the action. In working with organizations, I have found that active reflection consistently separates those that are able to sustain their agility from those that are agile on occasion or merely by accident.

Longtime agility leaders integrate reflection into their daily activities and create time to think about what they were doing when they were most agile. By taking note of what worked, they can more easily pinpoint the actions they should continue.

At DePaul University's School for New Learning, where I oversee our Center to Advance Education for Adults, we conducted a yearlong collaborative inquiry based on the question, "What if every encounter were a learning encounter?" We found that by intentionally keeping this question at the forefront of our formal and informal learning experiences, we increased the quality of our reflection and learning. In other words, when we consciously considered the possibility that every encounter might be a learning encounter, we found that more often than not, it was!

Agile entities of all sizes adopt an attitude of learning because they know they must. In rapidly changing circumstances those who rely solely on past experience, knowledge, and preconceptions without incorporating new and sometimes disconfirming knowledge and experience severely limit their capacity to respond effectively to the current reality. Seminal organizational thinker Karl Weick has studied many teams' and organizations' responses in life-or-death situations. In his analysis of one of the worst wildfires in history, the 1949 Mann Gulch disaster that killed sixteen firefighters, Weick asserted that many lives could have been saved if the men had not held on to their belief that they were fighting a familiar, routine fire despite rapidly changing conditions.[24] From the tragedy, Weick extracted universal wisdom for agility: "In a fluid world, wise people know that they don't fully understand what is happening right now, because they have never seen precisely this event before."[25]

The agility shift, of course, requires that you not only prioritize and practice reflection in the moment, but that you prioritize time to reflect-on-action once you have some distance from it. You will begin to make reflection a personal habit and part of your organizational culture as you experiment with the Make Shift Happen practices that follow.

Make Shift Happen

Attune to the Dynamic Present Moment

Expand your capacity to reflect in the midst of action by attending and attuning to what is happening in the dynamic present moment.

Sometimes when things are going well, we have an inclination to let our guards down and stop reflecting.

Improv theater troupes work hard to keep their shows fresh, because it can be easy to fall into variations of routines and characters that got laughs in the past. A team of improvisers at Chicago-based

ComedySportz thwarted this seductive pull by intentionally shifting their reflection on the success of the evening's performance. Matt Elwell, executive director of the newly rebranded CSz Worldwide, longtime improv player, and corporate trainer, shared, "In improvisation, we're not afraid of mistakes. [We have learned that...] if we react to a mistake with judgment and contempt, we're taking the scene downhill. We try to react to it mindfully and say, 'How can we spin it? How can we turn it?' It makes me think of what we call grounding, which is just this idea of I'm on stage, something isn't working, I start to get that feeling of being in my head and judging my performance and I choose to reconnect with my body...and come back to the current moment."[26] Instead of focusing on how much the audience laughed, the group at Comedy-Sportz shifted their focus to the degree of whole-person presence they experienced in the moment, and used that mindfulness to be more in tune with their fellow actors. This enabled the actors to continuously challenge themselves rather than plateauing with stale routines.

Be Curious, Not Critical

Make the intentional shift from criticizing "what is" to being curious about "what could be."

Curiosity drives new learning and reflection. Without it, even if we notice something unexpected we may not be curious enough to pay attention to it, consider the root cause, and learn from the experience. Curiosity motivates us to read journals outside our field, attend conferences, network with new colleagues, hear fresh perspectives, and experiment with new strategies. All of these practices further support agility.

Those who lead with criticism quickly shut down the possibility for constructive reflection and miss out on opportunities to increase their agility. Criticism leads to blame; blame leads to defensiveness; defensiveness shuts down learning. Consider the differences between the quality of reflection that is generated by the statement, "Our response time to customer complaints is dismal!" and the question, "I wonder how we might improve our response time to customer complaints?" Shift your language to provoke your own and others' curiosity.

Part One Summary

Organizations that make and sustain results from their agility shift come in all sizes, and span industries and continents. They have in common the understanding that agility is their most essential competitive advantage, and to sustain this advantage they know they must intentionally foster each of the dynamics introduced in this section. They know that agile organizations weave a Relational Web and are relevant, responsive, resilient, resourceful, and reflective. In Part Two you will learn to maximize the role of your leaders, teams, entire organization, and ecosystem to make and sustain your agility shift.

PART TWO

Making the Agility Shift at All Levels of the System

CHAPTER FOUR

Becoming an Agile Leader: Empowering Everyone to Be Agile

One Saturday morning not too long ago, a weekend facilities manager at UPS was making his rounds through the near-empty building. In addition to overseeing the facility, he was on call for occasional requests to adjust the heat or AC and to manage various facility vendors. As he walked through the automotive department, he heard a phone ringing and ringing on an employee's desk. Though the call had little chance of being related to his responsibilities, he picked it up. On the other end of the phone was a frantic mother searching for a missing wedding dress for her daughter's wedding the following day. Apparently, the bridal shop had mislabeled the package and it was stuck somewhere in the system. The facilities manager responded, "Well, ma'am, I take care of the building but I will see what I can do." After a few phone calls, he located the dress in the district, had it dug out of the storage trailer, and had it couriered to the bride in time for the wedding. As the facility manager demonstrated, to make the agility shift, we also need to shift our concept of leadership.

The conventional theory of leadership dates back to 1776 and Scottish economist Adam Smith's *The Wealth of Nations*, as well as to long-standing military tradition, from which, not incidentally, much of the language and theory of strategy derives. While times have changed, much of our leadership mind-set has not. Strict division of labor and control tactics were useful and even necessary in transitioning from the agricultural to the industrial age. Likewise, militaristic command was practical when enemies were known and predictable. However, these strategies are woefully lacking in more volatile times.

In the age of VUCA, the military has recognized the need to shift its mind-set and practices. Many businesses, inspired by agile methodologies, are shifting to self-organizing teams, where all members share responsibility for their performance as a whole. This is the leadership practiced by the UPS facilities manager. Had the UPS manager followed convention, that bride might still be waiting for her wedding dress. This may seem like a small, possibly even exceptional, customer service story—but what happens when this kind of leadership is not an exception, but the rule throughout the organization? Imagine an entire organization of people who lead for agility and deliver consistent results for their customers.

In changing contexts, everyone needs the competence, capacity, and confidence to lead in the moment, not just those whose titles, job descriptions, and compensation packages put them in traditional leadership positions. The agility shift that leaders make defines leadership not as power over others but as power to take action. This mind-set shift for leadership is one of empowerment and leadership of self. The ability to lead others is also important, but there is no place for the wish to control them.

In addition to promoting leading by doing, the agility shift calls for leading by following, or followership. While this may seem like the opposite of leading, as "being a follower" often has a negative connotation, nothing could be further from the truth. It takes maturity and knowledge to know when to take the backseat and let someone else shine. This capacity is never more visible than within a jazz ensemble.[1] Agile leaders are attuned to where the energy is flowing and where momentum is building and, when needed, they know how to slip into a supporting role and keep the rhythm for those who are in the spotlight. Just as fluidly, they step out in front when it serves the needs of the client and business.

A leadership mind-set for agility is the first step toward creating agile and responsive organizations.

> The best networking technology and flexible organizational systems, processes, and structures will have little impact on overall organizational agility if the individuals who interact with them do not have the right mind-set.

No one had to tell the UPS facilities manager to pick up the phone that Saturday, or to go the extra mile to track down the missing wedding dress; no one told Umpqua's branch manager to open her location the morning after the blizzard; and no one should have to tell you or your colleagues when and how to act when an issue or opportunity arises. Your organization's success depends on the degree to which each and every employee leads by taking responsibility for your results. The Make Shift Happen practices below show you how.

Make Shift Happen

Take Responsibility for Your Relational Web

Attend and attune to the health of your Relational Web in the same way you approach your physical health: with wellness strategies that support long-term energy, strength, and mobility.

The UPS facility manager was not a hero because he picked up the phone that day; he was a hero because he had woven a Relational Web and knew whom to call to solve the case of the missing dress. It is no surprise to discover that executives with the greatest number of social ties are also the most successful. In fact, a study of 673 supply chain managers showed that those who used their ties to discuss issues with other groups were paid better, had better performance evaluations, and were more likely to be promoted.[2] To better understand the value of these ties, we must go a little deeper. These supply chain managers did not simply exchange business cards at a networking event or connect with others via LinkedIn; they actively used their ties to exchange ideas and resources.

Other studies have shown similar results. Researchers Rob Cross and Andrew Parker of IBM's Knowledge and Organizational Performance Forum discovered that the key distinction between high performers and others was not their use of technology or expertise but the size and diversity of their personal networks: "Whom you know has a significant impact on what you come to know, because relationships are critical for obtaining information, solving problems, and learning how to do your work."[3]

Cross and Parker found another distinguishing characteristic of high performers: they served as "energy hubs" for others. An energy hub is someone others consistently identify as giving them energy in their collaborations. This energy is contagious. When we experience generative conversations, interactions, and collaborations, we become the best version of ourselves—our creative, thoughtful, curious, passionate, and optimistic selves. When others encounter this self, it in turn brings out the best in them—all the more reason to connect and build with others who have this energy, and to expand and diversify your Relational Web.

Give Permission to Play

Model, recognize, and coach others to play with new ideas, perspectives, roles, and resources.

Throughout my years helping teams and individuals build their competence, capacity, and confidence to think on their feet and trust their innate creativity, I witnessed the power of the "Permission Giver." The person who played this role was often another colleague who took the risk to share a "crazy" idea, challenge the prevailing thinking, or even be a little silly. Once permission is given, others are emboldened to step a little further out of their comfort zones and join in. In this way, agile leaders play an essential role in fostering and cocreating a space in which team members can play with new ideas; they play the role of the Permission Giver. Anyone can play this role by:

- *Modeling* responsive and creative action and encouraging new ideas and perspectives

- *Recognizing* colleagues and others who are creative under pressure and fostering any of the five dynamics of agility
- *Coaching* colleagues and others who have opportunities to be more responsive and agile

In my research on those who expanded their capacity for agility and innovation, those who led by playing the role of the Permission Giver were often helping their colleagues discover competencies and capacities they never knew they had.[4]

Take Responsibility for Learning

Don't wait to be sent to a training class or assigned a coach.

Effective leaders take responsibility for their own learning; they seek out new information and develop new skills, perspectives, and experiences. Traditional approaches to learning assume a stable context; agile leaders know that they must learn continuously in constant preparation for ever-changing contexts and opportunities. My colleague Catherine Marienau, a professor at DePaul University's School for New Learning, starts most classes by asking her adult learners to take a moment to reflect on and write their answers to the following questions:

- How am I coming prepared to learn?
- How am I prepared to help others learn?
- What do I need to put in place to support my own and others' learning?

Experiment by reflecting on these questions yourself at the start of each day and notice what shifts. Consider a second round of reflection with agility in mind.

Leading with Whole-Person Agility

Self-leadership starts with the most basic awareness and understanding of the way we experience and respond to the world around us.

Without such understanding, we are at the mercy of our unconscious, habitual responses and the fight, freeze, or flight reactions of our reptilian brain. As a leader, especially one who is seeking to become more agile, you must work to understand how the human brain influences decisions. People have a natural inclination toward certain attitudes or emotions in various contexts, which leads to corresponding behavior. While we are hard wired for these reactions, they aren't always the best for supporting organizational progress or agility. These next few brain-based principles will help you become more aware and effective under stress, the first step in becoming a more agile leader.

• **The brain is a social organ.**[5] This is good news. As introduced in Chapter 2, connecting with others, building relationships, and making sense of what is happening around us through relationships actually strengthens and grows the neurons, dendrites, and synaptic connections that support agility. Interaction is exercise for the brain. The social nature of the brain means we are wired to attune to what others are thinking and feeling.[6] When social groups become too comfortable with their beliefs, perspectives, and ideas they can either overtly or covertly impede fresh thinking and novel approaches to opportunities and obstacles alike. The more you exercise your brain by connecting and building your Relational Web, the more fit you will be to creatively and effectively respond to the unexpected and unplanned. The social nature of the human brain, by design, enhances our ability to cooperate and coordinate, an ability that is key to our survival. Beyond this most basic and essential value, the social nature of our brain guides us to connect with others to share resources and ideas, the fuel for adaptation and innovation.

• **The brain's first priority is survival.** The reptilian brain is responsible for our physical survival. In addition to maintaining our basic bodily functions of breathing, heartbeat, and metabolism, it is the seat of our most visceral fight or flight response. Once triggered, these responses can cause us to quickly lose our ability to see the larger context of the situation, think creatively, and act intentionally and mindfully. With awareness, the rush of adrenaline, rapid heart rate, and heightened awareness that we experience in the midst of the unexpected also give us the much-needed sense of urgency that is essential to action, especially in time-sensitive contexts.

- **The brain hates uncertainty.** Because the brain's first priority is our physical survival, it tries to quickly reduce uncertainty and discern the level of potential threat; the goal is to see whether our survival will be best served by staying to fight or hightailing it out of the situation. The need to reduce uncertainty can lead us to move too quickly and make unwise and/or uniformed decisions based on the discomfort we experience in uncertainty. With awareness, uncertainty can prompt curiosity and lead us to question root causes as well as our assumptions and values, leading to new perspectives and approaches.

- **The brain learns by association.** In 1949, Canadian psychologist Donald Hebb proposed what has come to be known as the "fire together, wire together," or FTWT, theory of learning and memory. When two synapses "fire together" in the brain an association is formed. In essence, this means that much of our learning happens by association.[7] For example, we learn not to touch a hot stove because we experienced extreme pain from doing so in the past, or we come to associate certain foods with comfort. The synaptic connections, though unrelated, are simultaneous, and so the visual image of a flame or glowing burner (one set of synaptic connections) becomes associated with the experience of pain (a separate, but now related, set of synaptic connections).

- **Our learned associations protect us from having to use trial and error every time we encounter routine phenomena.** Once an association is made, we don't need to put our hand in the flame every time to test if it is safe. Once formed, these associations can also limit our ability to expand and explore beyond them, or may even become debilitating. People recovering from trauma need to learn to function in a world of potential triggers: sights, sounds, and smells that the reptilian brain has associated with threat, yet which are completely benign in new contexts. As we become increasingly aware of learned associations and their triggers, we can move away from our habitual reactions and toward an attitude of curiosity, where we open up more possibilities for being responsive.

The brain is located in the skull, but it is also part of our central nervous system (CNS), together with the spinal cord. The CNS is connected to the peripheral nervous system (PNS), the network of nerves that runs through our entire bodies, sensing and relaying information through the system for processing and meaning making. Understanding and appreciating cognition holistically is key to developing the capacity to lead with whole-person agility.

In the late '80s, cognitive linguist George Lakoff and his colleagues at University of California, Berkeley introduced the concept of embodied cognition, the idea that our minds and bodies are literally interconnected.[8] Our bodies influence what we think and our thoughts influence how our bodies behave. Lakoff illuminated the way we embody our organizing metaphors, which are ready-made stories we tell ourselves to understand what is happening. These embodied metaphors in turn influence the way we think and how we respond to the world around us. For example, studies have shown that, when asked to think about the future, participants tended to lean forward; inviting them to think about the past caused them to lean back slightly. In another study, participants perceived heavier objects as more valuable.[9]

> "The mind follows the body."   —Bessel van der Kolk[10]

Building on these and related discoveries, Dutch psychiatrist Bessel van der Kolk helps people recovering from trauma use embodied cognition to shift away from their habitual responses. For example, workshop participants are asked to assume a slumped-over position and then try saying, "I feel great! I'm very happy today!" Participants are then asked if they actually feel great (the answer invariably is "no"). Next, van der Kolk invites subjects to try the opposite: sit upright and adopt a happy expression while trying to feel bad (most have no luck).[11] Understanding how our brains and bodies habitually react to the stress of the unknown and unexpected, and becoming aware of our own embodied experiences, is empowering. The Make Shift Happen practices that follow can help restore awareness, and access to the full resources of our neocortex, where complex thinking and curiosity occur.

Make Shift Happen

Practice Whole-Person Leading

Invite others to engage their whole bodies in order to access their whole minds.

Understanding that cognition does not happen only from the neck up, but as a process involving the whole person and whole body, enables us to be more agile in the midst of complexity. When we are consciously aware of and engage our whole body, we have access to information, insights, and options that otherwise elude us. This kind of leadership is inspired by innovative educators who use multiple strategies to engage a wide array of learning styles and intelligences.[12] Such creative approaches are not only brain and whole-person friendly, they keep us engaged in continuous learning with the regular invitation to shift to new learning modes and into novel (and more memorable) experiences.

Agile leaders understand the importance of keeping their colleagues engaged and nimble, and are not afraid to experiment with a range of embodied strategies. One of the ways I help leaders make this shift in my work with organizations is by inviting them to disrupt their meeting routines, get up out of their chairs, and physicalize their project status, sales goals, or new ideas. This may sound risky, or even a bit crazy, at first. However, leaders who model and encourage such whole-person engagement will be rewarded with greater access to fresh ideas and perspectives when it counts most.

Practice Presence

Regularly attune to what you are experiencing and thinking to be able to shift from simply reacting to responding effectively under stress.

Agile leaders are self-aware and present. They cannot afford to be hijacked by habitual responses or mindless reactions. Ellen Langer describes mindfulness, "the process of actively noticing things."[13] Her four decades of research on practicing mindfulness have made the concept popular from Silicon Valley to Wall Street.[14] Tara Bennett-Goleman, in her book *Emotional Alchemy,* shares how practices borrowed from mindfulness meditation can help us become more aware of signs that our reptilian brain and limbic system are triggering reactive responses, which she refers to as schemas:[15]

- At the first moment of awareness of a triggering response, intentionally block the trigger with a positive response (ideally a contradicting thought coupled with an embodied behavior).
- Challenge your automatic thoughts with a reality check ("Is what I think is going on really going on, or am I making up a story that fits my past experiences?").
- Intentionally shift the unpleasant embodied experience by changing your stance, expression, and/or location (for example, by literally stepping away from the source of the trigger).
- Do something constructive and proactive to change the pattern that has been triggered (this could be changing your language, behavior, and/or habituated response).
- Practice being aware of and consciously changing your triggered patterns at every opportunity.

Don't Go it Alone

Shift from the Western notion of leadership as a solo venture. Not only is there safety in numbers, there is often less anxiety and clearer, more creative thinking. It turns out that when we feel part of a group, something larger than ourselves, we tend to persevere longer in the face of uncertainty and adversity, and we experience less anxiety.[16] As described in last chapter's example of the difference most of us experience between getting lost alone or with a companion, intentionally tapping your Relational Web in anticipation of, or in the midst of, the unexpected and unplanned dramatically increases the chances that you will be able to think clearly rather than be at the mercy of your reactive responses.

Reappraise the Situation

While mindfulness practices initially require you to step out of the moment, with intention and regular practice you will soon find yourself becoming more aware and responsive in the heat of the moment.

Jeremy Jamieson and his colleagues at Harvard studied two groups of students who were preparing to take the GRE (Graduate Record Exam), necessary for admission to many graduate programs. One group was told that students who experience anxiety during test taking tend to do better on the test, while the other group was told nothing. Perhaps not surprisingly, the group who perceived stress as a positive performed significantly better on the test. Jamieson calls this the shift from worrier to warrior, more formally known as *cognitive reappraisal*.[17] Improvisers in the arts make similar mind-set shifts to be effective on stage when they must respond to the many unexpected twists in a performance. Improvisers call the surprises that occur during a performance "gifts," and open them with delight and positive expectation.

Agile Leaders Are Learning Agile

Learning agility is the most important leadership competence for success in changing contexts. Two different research teams—Michael Lombardo and Robert Eichinger,[18] and Adam Mitchinson and Robert Morris[19]—pioneered this idea after studying the success stories of hundreds of executives across industries.[20] The executives they studied had a common thread running through their successful careers: each had developed and demonstrated something the researchers came to call learning agility. It is made up of two interrelated dynamics: the ability to learn in the midst of action and the ability to draw on prior learning and experience for success in unfamiliar contexts (transferable learning).

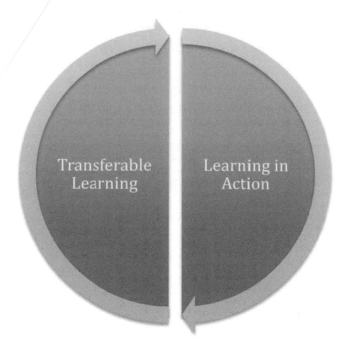

Leaders who possess competence, capacity, and confidence in these dynamics are more successful and are more likely to deliver results for their organizations. However, learning agility is not simply the ability to think on your feet. Learning agility is the ability to access and apply lessons learned in one context to another. In 1988, management researchers Morgan McCall, Michael Lombardo, and Ann Morrison studied the significant learning experiences of more than 190 executives. They found that the key to success within a complex organization was the ability to manage something new without having to master it first. In other words, successful managers did not need to go through lengthy training or have prior experience in a similar role; they possessed the competence, capacity, and confidence to access and translate relevant prior learning, which allowed them to learn and adapt on the job.

My friend Ann Johnson exemplifies this dimension of learning agility. It has been many years since her days as a stage manager in regional theater, a role that requires significant agility. A good stage manager must be highly detail oriented to keep an entire creative process on schedule, all while responding to the competing needs of the actors, director, designers, production crew, and, yes, even the audience. Though it has been a while since she played that role, Ann finds that she regularly taps the skills and knowledge she developed in her stage manager years for her current work as an event planner. Event planning requires management of hundreds of details and the ability to deal with a range of egos and oft-stressed personalities. Like a stage manager, an event planner must be able to respond to countless unexpected events and pull everything together on the day of "performance."

Unfortunately, the ability to tap prior experience and think creatively on your feet is not as common a trait as we might hope. As anyone who has worked with an ineffective leader can confirm, competence in one's current role is a weak predictor of potential for success in a new, more challenging role. According to research published by the Corporate Leadership Council, only 30 percent of an organization's high performers have the potential to rise to and succeed in broader, senior-level, critical positions.[21] A study by the Korn Ferry Institute identified learning agility as the top-ranking predictor of leadership success. However, the researchers estimated that only 15 percent of the workforce is "highly learning agile."[22]

As a side note, it is interesting that this finding tracks with the 13 percent of the workforce said to be "actively engaged" according to a recent Gallup poll.[23] This is likely not a coincidence. Without engagement there will be no agility; without agility there will be no engagement.

Leaders who understand these principles are starting to make learning agility a key strategic priority. However, this type of agility is not something easily acquired in a classroom. The next set of Make Shift Happen practices helps you lead from a mind-set of learning agility.

Make Shift Happen

Hold Your Mental Models Lightly

Make it a regular practice to question the assumptions and beliefs that guide your thinking and actions. Intentionally "try on" other perspectives to see if they open up fresh ideas and courses of action.

Whether we are aware of them or not, we all view the world through our mental models, or schemas. These frameworks and beliefs influence what we see, what we pay attention to, our understanding of what is happening, and ultimately the course of action we take. Agile leaders are aware of their mental models and are able to hold them lightly, understanding that, although they may have been in a similar situation before, the current situation must be viewed with fresh eyes.

Adopt an Attitude of Inquiry

Intentionally shift your attitude to one of inquiry. Ask one more question. Probe for underlying assumptions and biases. Set an expectation of new learning in each interaction.

Curiosity cannot be taught, but it can certainly be killed. Without a playspace where curiosity can thrive, it is all too easy to fall into the comfort of routine and assumptions learned from conditions that no longer exist. Agile leaders assume the context is changing and will continue to change. Rather than fear it, they actively inquire about its nature and the opportunities it holds. To foster creativity within your organization, lead by encouraging your colleagues to ask questions.

Cultivate Confidence

Seek out experiences that take you out of your comfort zone and require you to stretch your skills or scope.

One of the most consistent comments I hear from clients, as well as my adult graduate students, is that the biggest value of trying something new is the increased confidence they feel afterward. Stepping outside your comfort zone may be scary, but that time spent thinking on your feet will change your mind-set long after the experience ends. Stretch experiences will differ from one leader to the next, but the essential ingredient is that the experience provide an opportunity to succeed in unfamiliar territory. As a leader, you can bolster others' confidence by challenging them to push their boundaries.

Being a truly agile leader isn't about having power over others— it's about taking responsibility for your own empowerment and empowering others. We're in the midst of a shift in perspective from a command-and-control philosophy to one in which widespread decision-making power ensures that things get done quickly and effectively. Throughout this chapter I highlighted aspects of the leadership mind-set shift necessary to become a more agile individual. In the next chapter, you will learn how you can make this shift with your teams and work groups.

CHAPTER FIVE

Building the Agile Team

The 1980s and '90s were the heyday of "the team" and all the now well-worn slogans and sports metaphors that came with it. Today, the language of teamwork has lost its luster, though in reality small groups still do much of the work. What has changed is that these groups are now often informal, temporary, or spontaneous. Whether you call it a team, workgroup, committee, department, hallway meeting, coffee break, cluster, or crew, a work group must be able to be effective in the face of obstacles and opportunity if your organization is to be successful.

> "If the future is uncertain, best learn to improvise."
>
> —Mary Crossan and Roderick White[1]

For the purposes of this chapter, I will call these groups "teams," but I have a very different kind of metaphor in mind: the improv team.

Agility Lessons from Improv Teams

I worked as a theater director for years, which gave me the opportunity to see agile teams in action day in and day out. I saw firsthand how improvisation helps expand the capacity for agility and the ability to generate ideas for new material. An improv team made up of seasoned and novice improvisers continuously hones its capacity to engage with the dynamic present, the site of discovery and action. Improv team members work without a script, think on their feet, and quickly shift roles and agendas as the scene unfolds to its unpredictable yet often delightful conclusion. Improv teams place their agility capacity and competence above all others and continuously and intentionally work to expand it.

Rather than being like sports teams, agile business teams are more akin to improv troupes. Agile teams make a shift from executing according to a predefined playbook to working without any script at all, adhering only to a few agreed-upon givens. For improvisers, these initial givens are often provided by the audience; for business players, they are set by the client and available resources. In both contexts, players co-create with the expectation that more givens will be discovered in the midst of the fast-paced collaboration.

The agility shift is characterized by project teams and ad hoc collaborations that, like improv teams, are often thrown together at a moment's notice without time for lengthy introductions. There is no chance to find out where everyone went to school, to swap résumés, or to discover each person's particular talents or behavioral style. Improvisers do not stand in the wings planning what to do when they start, who will take on what role, where they will set the scene, or how long the piece will last. Such formalities are not just a waste of time but an impediment to creativity, an obstacle to the discoveries they will make playing in the dynamic present. From years of watching players in smoky cabarets (before smoking was banned in public spaces) and rehearsing in musty church basements, I distilled the secrets of the agile team. These practices do not diminish the value of onboarding and other formal orientation strategies. No matter how oriented you are to an organization, its culture, and its people, you will encounter new players and situations every day that require you to improvise. The Make Shift Happen practices that follow will help your team function like a seasoned improv team.

Make Shift Happen

Identify Your Givens

At each opportunity, check that your team is working with the same understanding of the givens.

Sometimes improvisers begin a scene or game with a suggestion or two from the audience. Sometimes the suggestion is quite general—a phrase, pet peeve, or made-up movie title. Other teams may start by asking the audience to suggest a "who" (characters), "what" (event or theme), and "where" (physical setting for the scene). These givens are the first pieces of information agreed on and, more importantly, accepted by the players. They help structure the play, set boundaries within which the players' creativity can flourish, and bring some order to the chaos that is sure to unfold.

Agile teams are sometimes able to get their givens in advance, though just as often the givens must be discovered in the heat of performance. Each new discovery, piece of client input, project requirement, budget or technology limitation, unexpected occurrence, or setback becomes a new given within which agile teams must continue to play. Success depends on sensing and responding to these shifting givens as they are discovered. Successful work teams that identify, agree upon, and adapt to changing givens are most successful at playing within them. The agility shift depends on collaborators who regularly check in with one another and their clients to confirm they are working within the same givens, and who make adjustments if and when those givens change.

Agree to Agree

Once you have identified your givens, agree to them to speed your response and innovation rate.

Stage improvisers have no time to work out their differences or to wage power struggles. Before they ever set foot on stage, they have an agreement—each player agrees to agree with, and more importantly, accept whatever the audience gives him and to build on it. He also accepts whatever choice his fellow players make and builds on it. Finally, all players accept whatever game rules are imposed and play within them. No matter what happens, the players know they won't be hung out to dry. Failing to agree shatters the team's foundation, destroying the forward motion of the collaboration.

The players do not choose the direction of the scene; they accept the gifts of discovery and find the most interesting opportunity within each one as the scene unfolds. At first blush, it might seem that such lack of choice coupled with the willingness to accept whatever is offered would set the stage for disaster. Yet these are the two crucial ingredients of improv success.

Anthony Holland, one of the early members of Second City, reflected, "One of the reasons so many people who try to do improv go wrong is that they aren't in agreement…'This coffee tastes good,' [says one person] and the other person says, 'What coffee? It's tea.' That's how to kill an improv."[2]

The truth is that you may have little more choice in your workplace givens than do your improvising counterparts. In a competitive marketplace you do not choose "who" your collaborators are or what role they play, "what" event or reason brings you together, or even "where" you are going to collaborate. You do not choose who is on the other end of the line when the phone rings. You rarely choose your immediate supervisor or team members. Success depends on your ability to work with any personality in any context. This is improvisation.

Agreeing to agree and accept is the foundation for trust between the players. Trust is the foundation for the shared success of agile teams.

Practice Gift Giving

Be intentional in the gifts you give as a team player, and recognize and reward those gifts that are particularly valuable to the collaboration.

Once all the players identify and agree on the givens, they can begin swapping gifts. I must accept the gift you give me (your idea, new discovery, unexpected twist) as though it is the most wonderful thing I have ever received, and then reciprocate by giving you something even more delightful in return.

The most sought-after improv players are those who generously give their ideas, discoveries, and wonderful and weird personalities to the co-created scene. Their fellow players know that even if they start to dry up, they can count on these players to give a gift that, when accepted and built upon, will get the scene rolling again. When you give gifts in an agile team, you are debunking the trope "there is no 'I' in teamwork" and performing what organizational psychologist Philip Mirvis calls "collective individuality."[3] This is the sweet spot where diversity, coordination, communication, and collaboration converge. Agile teams celebrate the unique contributions of each player and take responsibility to accept and build on the gifts each contributor offers.

Find the Game

Practice finding the game in your agile team by identifying and amplifying patterns of interaction as you play.

Making the agility shift means adopting an attitude of playfulness and discovery. You must enjoy the adventure of finding and playing the game, saying "yes!" to it, and then building on the discoveries your fellow players make. Improvisers sometimes call the discovery of their givens and patterns of interaction "finding the game."

All games have some basic rules that the players must agree upon to have a successful and challenging game. Aside from agreeing to agree, improvisers have a few rules they start with. The fun is in discovering the rules along the way as the game reveals itself by way of a central theme or repeating pattern that can be amplified and influenced through play. You know how to do this from your childhood games, many of which were made up right on the spot.

I watched Jane, a party guest all of six years old, demonstrate "finding the game" perfectly in her "Star Girls" tag game, made up in the moment using the available resources. I was there to assist the birthday girl, Zoe's, parents with the planned activities at the Chicago Children's Museum. Turns out, the guests needed little help finding the fun. Upon entering, Jane's wrist was stamped with a red shooting star. "Star Girls! Star Girls!" she yelled. Within moments she had "found the game" to engage the other early arrivals. She brought her enthusiasm into the room as she inspected the other guests' wrists. Moments later, girls were running around squealing with delight as they played the "Star Girls" game. The rules were simple: whoever is "it" chases the others and tries to touch her star to the next girl's. A successful tag means everyone gets to yell "Star Girls!" The parents sprinkled around the room are "safe." None of the players hesitated to accept the rules of "Star Girls." There was no negotiation or resistance from any of the new players as they arrived at the party. They immediately saw and heard how much fun the others were having and couldn't wait to find the game and join in.

Unlike enthusiastic birthday party guests, adults sometimes get bogged down before they even begin to play. They either have no interest in finding the game, are in disagreement over the givens, or make assumptions based on their own interpretation of the rules and are caught off guard when they discover that the other players made entirely different assumptions. Rather than look for the patterns of interaction, adults are known to disrupt the patterns before they even emerge.

Agile teams start by naming the current "givens": "Here's what we know so far..." You can fill in the blanks with as many of the givens you and your collaborators can name. Now, invite your collaborators to answer this question with you: "Where do we want to be by the end of this meeting?" Now you have your point of focus to generate ideas, define or solve a problem, and/or implement a plan *in the dynamic present.* Whoever offers the first idea sets the pattern of gift giving in motion. With intention, your team will notice patterns as they emerge and play with their possibilities. Not only will you be surprised by how much more rapidly you generate ideas, find solutions, and respond to changes, the level of energy you generate will keep your team motivated and engaged to achieve (and often exceed) your agreed-upon objectives. When you make the shift to agility, identifying the givens and finding the game becomes part of the way you do business.

Agility Lessons from High-Stakes Teams

Lessons learned from successful agile teams working in high-stakes, high-stress, and even high-risk circumstances reinforce that agile teams in any context must have both the required competence and capacity for:

Continuous learning. Teams must be able to quickly become aware of, assess, and often reassess new information in real time. This includes the capacity to drop prior plans, agendas, and preconceptions as they become obsolete and respond to the situation at hand.

Fluid communication. Agile organizations have open channels of communication across job functions and levels of authority. Critical new information can emerge at any level of the system at any time. Those who receive or perceive the data must have the confidence and competence to share it with the appropriate stakeholder.

Context creation. As introduced in the previous chapter, playspace is the serious business of creating the context in which people are free to play with new ideas, take on new roles, create more play in the system, and engage in improvisation. This is not the funny-hats-and-games type of playspace. It is about creating a context in which people are free (and empowered) to respond in the moment to an urgent customer or business need, rather than constrained because it is not in their job description.

Your job most likely does not include storming drug houses or shooting big-budget movies, but we can all learn some valuable lessons from seeing how SWAT teams and film crews are able to be effective when the stakes are at their highest.

Scenario One: After months of rigorous preparation, a SWAT team surrounded the suspected drug house. The team had studied the suspects and the floor plan. They had rehearsed their strategy several times. On their commander's signal, they burst through the door only to discover that the interior walls of the house had been rearranged. Freeze this image in your mind.

Scenario Two: A film crew was in the middle of shooting a high-budget horror movie. They had rented out a large, old mansion and began the day filming a scene on the top floor. In this scene a very large man was to be attacked and then fall backward into a full hot tub. What they hadn't planned for was just how much water would be displaced when that large man fell into the tub. Water quickly cascaded over the sides and began dripping through the ceiling of the rooms below, shorting out the electricity for the entire building. Freeze frame.

The teams in both these scenarios, which were studied by researchers Beth Bechky and Gerardo Okhuysen, were ultimately able to succeed because they had already made the shift necessary to respond to the unexpected and remain creative under pressure.[4] In addition to developing these abilities, both the SWAT team and the film crew made and sustained their agility shift by (1) creating a Relational Web, (2) expecting role elasticity and learning agility, and (3) developing resource awareness. You will discover just how these teams adjusted and responded with the Make Shift Happen practices that follow.

Make Shift Happen

Weave Your Team's Relational Web in the Moment

Provide opportunities for interaction that are not tied to immediate tasks, projects, or urgent deadlines. From the start of your collaboration, interact with the expectation that the web has and will be woven as you work and play together.

Whether teams have been together for years or have been thrown together quickly to respond to a new opportunity, Relational Webs provide the interpersonal and resource connections to make sense of what is happening and respond effectively. Just like stage improvisers, members of agile and sometimes ad hoc teams do not always have the luxury of weaving their Relational Web through weeks of teambuilding exercises, off-sites, and strategy sessions. They must come together with an expectation that everyone on the team has the necessary level of training, experience, and creativity to be able to respond to any and all obstacles and opportunities that cross their paths.

While some members of these teams may have worked together on other projects (as film crew members often do) or special operations (such as SWAT teams), their projects rarely afford them the opportunity to develop their Relational Web through long-term, day-in-and-day-out interactions. Their secret is that they arrive on site with the relational mind-set and behave as if the necessary ties are already intact, which allows them to quickly access the collective knowledge of the group. This attitude and behavior effectively enacts team agility on the spot, turning expectation into reality.

In my years producing and directing theater I often relied on the wider Relational Web to quickly assemble production teams and find replacement members and special talent. When my special effects designer moved away weeks before opening night, we found the perfect person at the School of the Art Institute of Chicago, just a few degrees of separation away. I always knew that I could count on anyone who was a respected member of the wider network to be an effective player from the moment he arrived. You have likely experienced the power of your own Relational Web if you have recruited collaborators based on shared credentials, training programs, education, or other past experiences.

Warning: This is not an invitation to stay within your affinity groups as you assemble your teams, a practice that can lead to a singular, limited perspective and lack of diversity. It is a reminder of the importance of creating a mind-set and practices that reinforce the Relational Web of your team.

Communicate and Coordinate in the Dynamic Present

First, make team communication and coordination expectations explicit. Second, model, practice, and recognize them.

The shift from information to interaction introduced in chapter 1 is especially key to agile team success for those whose lives depend on their ability to rapidly make sense of changing conditions. Flight crews are one such team. These crews often assemble shortly before a flight, yet they share responsibility for the safety and well-being of hundreds of passengers and millions of dollars' worth of equipment. In his study of effective flight crews, Robert Ginnett discovered that, in the age of increasingly automated cockpit controls, flight safety is more dependent on crew members' ability to communicate and coordinate with one another than it is on aviation skills and knowledge. Cockpit resource management (CRM) is now the international standard for crew training. It includes guidelines to ensure that each crew member arrives prepared to enact any of these four exchanges:

1. I need to talk to you.
2. I listen to you.
3. I need you to talk to me.
4. I expect you to talk to me.[5]

Such behaviors and specific practices allow flight and film crews, as well as SWAT teams, to make the agility shift that creates and reinforces their Relational Web, enabling them to quickly assess and adapt to the unexpected.

Expect Role Elasticity and Learning Agility

Shift your mind-set from relying on assigned roles to expecting role elasticity.

Members of an agile team know they must be willing to do whatever it takes to get the job done. Each of the agility success stories I've highlighted hinges on the capacity of each member to quickly shift roles and even agendas as the unexpected unfolds. UPS executives expect to shift to package sorting during crunch time; Umpqua Bank's universal associates expect to quickly shift from teller to loan officer to Internet café host. This type of role elasticity is expected and demands a companion competence and capacity for learning agility, introduced earlier.

The ability to think on their feet and quickly translate prior experience for use in unfamiliar situations enabled the SWAT team to quickly communicate with one another via eye contact and hand gestures, switch roles and strategy in seconds, and successfully complete their operation. A strong Relational Web, together with role elasticity and learning agility, also allowed the film crew to adapt quickly. On a film set, crew members rarely have only one specialty. In fact, it is not unusual to be on the prop crew one day and hanging lights the next. While they couldn't continue shooting the hot tub scene on the day the tub overflowed, the crew was able to quickly review the shot list, find the one dry room in the house, and continue shooting. They were able to regroup quickly because they, like all agile teams, had the final Make Shift strategy in place.[6]

Develop Resource Awareness

Intentionally create opportunities for expanding team resource awareness.

Agile team members are aware of available resources and are able to improvise with them as necessary. When the electricity went out due to water damage in the midst of the film shoot, it could have spelled disaster. Losing even a single day of filming means budget overruns, as well as the potential to lose the availability of tightly scheduled talent. Because the crew was aware of their available resources (an on-site generator) and had the competence to quickly set it up, they lost very little filming time. By working with their available resources and talent—their givens—and by having an expectation of role elasticity and learning agility, they were up and running again after only a short break.[7]

Your team can't be resourceful if it doesn't know what resources it has. Teams and entire organizations are doing away with information silos. For example, the product development department may be working on something that would wow potential clients and help you win their business, but you can't use that as a selling point if you don't know about it. Organizations benefit from improving interdepartmental communication and educating all team members on resources.

Lessons from Agile Development Teams

In a 2001 event that is now the stuff of legend, a group of software developers, including Extreme Programming mentors Bob Martin and Jeff Sutherland, gathered at a Utah ski resort for a few days of recreation and reflection. Over the course of many conversations, a common theme emerged: all were frustrated with the cumbersome and ineffective process of traditional software development that prioritized project documentation over innovative working software and processes and tools over individuals and interactions. Martin summarized the sentiments that had brought them all together: "We all enjoyed working with people who shared compatible goals and values based on mutual trust and respect, promoting collaborative, people-focused organizational models, and building the types of professional communities in which we would want to work."[8] By the end of their time together the group had drafted what is now known as "The Agile Manifesto," a list of guiding principles that set the stage for a major shift in the way software developers, and now many project teams, get things done. In the next several pages, I describe the most groundbreaking aspects of this shift.

From Waterfall to Sprints

Prior to wider adoption of agile project management methods, most software was developed using a "waterfall" approach. This approach is drawn from (and more suited to) manufacturing processes. With waterfall, as much input as possible is gathered at the start of the project (usually from the client). From there, the entire process is outlined with specific steps and predetermined outcomes. While it sounds wonderfully logical and efficient in theory, in practice it is inefficient and limits team agility. In fact, the most common outcome of the waterfall method is a product or service that is significantly over budget and long overdue.[9]

The waterfall approach also limits innovation. When the priority is getting from one level of the waterfall to the next, rather than continuous learning through iterations, the team has little ability to discover and respond to new developments, especially those that impact some of the early-stage work. Or, in the words of James Johnston, project manager at Mightybytes, "If a client wants to make changes, it can be quite time consuming and costly to revisit something that's already built."[10] In other words, it's not easy to go back up a waterfall.

> We've examined plenty of successful projects and few, if any, delivered what was planned in the beginning, yet they succeeded because the development team was agile enough to respond again and again to external changes.
>
> —Martin Fowler and Jim Highsmith, cocreators of "The Agile Manifesto," with the Agile Alliance[11]

Teams that adopt agile methodologies, such as those as at Ericsson and Mightybytes, have made the shift from waterfall to sprints. This shift is founded on the practice of continuous discovery and customer collaboration. Rather than asking the customer to step back after she has provided her initial project requirements and goals, the team invites her to continue on as an active member of the development team. Project work is then broken into short sprints, which often last two to four weeks. As described by Martin Fowler and Jim Highsmith, the focus here "is on satisfying the customer through early and continuous delivery of valuable software."[12]

Like their improv actor counterparts, agile developers welcome new discoveries and shifting client requirements. These things are accepted as "gifts" that seed innovation and effectiveness. Stage improvisers know they are in trouble if they begin a scene thinking they know how it should end. This is because they are working an agenda and are unable to make fresh discoveries in the dynamic present. Agile developers have a similar relationship to "a plan." If achieving the plan exactly as envisioned at the start of the project is the sole objective, they know they have already sacrificed the most compelling opportunity of the collaboration: innovation.

From Command and Control to Self-Organization

In the fast-paced life of new product or service development, there is no time to wait for direction or decisions from those in authority. In fact, agile teams abandon such distinctions. Instead, those doing the work decide what work gets done and how. It may sound radical at first, but in practice it is the most practical, efficient, and effective way to work. This does not mean agile teams are made up of rogue operators. Quite the opposite. Agile developers succeed by communicating and coordinating in the dynamic present.

With intentional practice, self-organization works within agile teams and can even work between teams. In their study of particle physicists distributed across 170 computing centers in thirty-four countries, Yingqin Zheng and his colleagues coined the term "collective agility" to describe the success of scientists working on a high-stakes project. They likened the scientists' capacity and competence to that of seasoned improvisers who fluidly shift and coordinate with each new discovery.[13]

From False Security to Anxious Confidence

Particle physicists and improvisers share something in common in addition to their capacity and competence: their success is characterized by the mind-set of what organizational psychologist Philip Mirvis terms "anxious confidence."[14] Rather than working with a false sense of security, particle physicists are effective because they are anxious. They know that at any given moment they are likely to encounter the unexpected and unplanned. At the same time, they are confident because they know they have clearly established goals (or givens, in the language of improvisation); have woven a Relational Web made up of the best and brightest in their field; have a track record (either individually or collectively) of success; and have the communication, collaboration, and coordination competence to respond to new developments as they emerge.

> "Agility is all about trusting in one's ability to respond to unpredictable events more than trusting in one's ability to plan ahead for them."
>
> —"The Agile Manifesto"[15]

The creative tension between anxiety and confidence delivers each player, whether his stage is the laboratory, conference room, client meeting, or late night cabaret stage, into the ever-important dynamic present moment. These players are ready to respond to obstacles and opportunities, and they are ready to see obstacles as opportunities. These two dimensions of the agile team combine to create collective individuality.[16]

You don't need to develop software to benefit from the lessons of agile methodology. Organizations like Ericsson are making the agility shift by fostering the agile mind-set and extending the lessons of agile methodology throughout their organizations.

Make Shift Happen

Practice Rapid Prototyping: Fail Faster, Learn Quicker

Shift your project strategy into collaborative sprints and practice continuous learning.

Agile development is a form of rapid prototyping. Each project is broken into two- to four-week "sprints," with the goal of getting working software into the hands of the client for testing and experimentation by the end of each period. Because testing and feedback are integrated into the entire process, unlike the more linear waterfall approach, agile developers fail faster and learn more quickly. Discovering and responding to bugs and issues, as well as to new opportunities along the way, is much easier and more cost effective than responding shortly before or, worse, after public release. If you need evidence of this, just look at the initial launch of the healthcare.gov website in the United States. The site was first developed using waterfall methodologies. Because it was not tested until days before the launch, the site was so full of bugs and glitches that it threatened to derail the president's signature initiative. How did the developers fix the site and rescue the rollout? By shifting to agile teams and strategies.

Agile software teams hold daily stand-up meetings in which they share their progress as well as any obstacles they are encountering. These meetings are called "stand-ups" because they are intentionally so brief that attendees literally stand up throughout. Stand-ups can be held in person or virtually. The sole focus of the meeting is to communicate, collaborate, and coordinate to keep the project moving forward. For agile teams, continuous learning, feedback, and failure are built into the process itself, not left until the very end when a final product is debuted for the client or until a postmortem review. Jeff Sutherland, founder of Scrum Inc., asks his agile teams three questions in his daily stand-ups:

- What did you do yesterday to help the team finish the sprint?
- What will you do today to help the team finish the sprint?
- What obstacles are getting in the team's way?[17]

These very brief stand-up meetings provide everyone on the team with the information and opportunity for continuous learning through this simple framework for communicating, collaborating, and coordinating.

Work at a Sustainable Pace and Capacity

Despite the sound of it, the sprint metaphor, with its focus on failing and learning quickly, is not a setup for rapid burnout. At least not when it is practiced well. Agile developers know they must be able to sustain their pace, attention, and engagement throughout the process. Olympic sprinters follow a disciplined training schedule that prioritizes rest and recovery as much as the actual race. An exhausted athlete has no more chance of winning than does a burned-out, frustrated, or disengaged team.

To foster a sustainable working pace and climate, agile development includes time for regular reflection on the process itself. At the end of each sprint, of which there may be many, agile teams ask another set of questions to help them improve and sustain their success:

- How can we work together better in the next sprint?
- What was getting in our way during the last one?
- What are the impediments that are slowing our velocity?[18]

These regular process reflections are also opportunities for a team happiness check. Sutherland saw a significant bump in business results when he began asking questions like, "What one thing would make you happier in the next sprint?"[19] The key to sustaining your agile team, of course, is not just asking the questions, but responding to the answers. LaTodd Williams, scrum master at Ericsson, counsels, "If you are not able to consistently meet the goals of each sprint, or your team is burning out, you need to do one of two things: (1) break your project into more manageable chunks and/or (2) expand the size of your team."[20]

Create an Agile Manifesto for Your Team

When that hearty band of software developers gathered in Utah, they shared the obstacles to working at the top of their talent. And they did so in a way that was both joyful and effective. Rather than letting their time together devolve into a gripe session, they used it to create a vision for a new way of working, one that is generative and sustainable. This vision, "The Agile Manifesto," triggered an agility shift across an industry and has inspired similar shifts for others who develop and execute projects for a wide range of internal and external clients.[21] I have referenced several of the principles of "The Agile Manifesto" in this chapter (see Appendix A for full manifesto). Here is your opportunity to consider which of them you might want to adopt or modify for your own team. What others might you add? The process of creating an "Agile Manifesto" for your own team and the conversations and commitments it will spur will go a long way toward helping you and your team make your own agility shift.

This chapter has shown how different types of teams shift their mind-set, as well as their behavior, to ensure team agility and effectiveness. Even if you don't think of yourself as being part of a team, I hope you discovered a number of Make Shift Happen practices that you can apply in your next collaboration. Keep this mind-set as we move on to the next chapter and an even wider arena—the entire organization.

CHAPTER SIX

Co-Creating the Agile Organization

When it comes to agility, the distinctions between individual roles, teams, and organizations are less important than the collective capacity to respond to opportunities and challenges. All aspects of the system must be able to communicate, collaborate, and coordinate. Just as athletes cannot be competitive if they are strong and flexible everywhere but their right knee, an organization cannot compete if one of its components is ineffective, or if communication between team members has broken down.

Many agility strategies fail because they don't approach the shift with the human system in mind. World-class communication systems and access to resources will not compensate for a culture and climate that prioritizes comfort and control over learning and innovation. These capacities are rooted in human mind-sets, motivations, and behaviors.

For this reason, the entire human system must shift to one in which all are committed to constructing and reinforcing a culture within which responsive and innovative thinking and action thrive. In the next several pages we will zoom out for a wider-angle view of this system to discover the role your networks, organizational structure, and systems and processes play in enhancing or impeding agility, as well as how to improve each of these aspects for maximum organizational performance.

Organizations as Systems of Interaction

Whether you are a weekend warrior or a professional athlete, you know that before you participate in your chosen activity, you must first strengthen your core. Balance and stability radiate from core strength. Your organization is grounded in your unique core competencies (the skills, knowledge, and talent that drive your business success) and your robust Relational Web.

Agile leaders are shifting from thinking of their organization as a mechanistic system of efficient parts to a dynamic system of human interaction. In this shift, organizations become systems for organizing. Rather than static nouns, they become verbs brought to life each day through the networking activities of relating and interacting. This represents a significant mind-set shift, as the very word "organization" is rooted in a noun, the Greek word *organon*, meaning "tool." While agile organizations make a shift from nouns to verbs, they know the underlying purpose of organizing remains the same: to "Get Shit Done," as declared by the mug on the desk of Sally Anderson, Google's head of people development. And it must be done while leaving employees room to reflect, incubate, experiment, and innovate.

The agility shift means creating networks, structures, systems, and processes that support human interactions, rather than simply designing and implementing a system that enables mechanistic transactions. Lani Hayward, EVP of Creative Strategies reflected on how she and her colleagues at Umpqua Bank worked to sustain organizational agility as they doubled in size via a recent merger. "When culture breaks it is because people become disconnected from each other," she remarked at the time.[1] Organizational agility depends on a healthy culture, and a healthy culture depends on a strong Relational Web.

Weaving the Organizational Relational Web

If agility is your strategic priority, your organizational structure must enable effective interactions. If you are lucky enough to be reading this while building a new organization from the ground up, you have the enviable luxury of a fresh start. Architect Louis Sullivan popularized the philosophy "form follows function."[2] It makes sense that the organizational design must also follow its most essential function: effective interaction.

More likely you are reading this with an existing organization and inherited structure in mind. While you may not be able to radically redesign your organization from the ground up, the good news is that you can still make the agility shift by applying lessons learned from those who are creating networks, structures, systems, and processes to maximize existing resources.

Organizations are made up of countless individual Relational Webs, through which we each construct our sense of self, make meaning, and get things done. For most of us, our Relational Web extends to a range of social, professional, and recreational networks.

These connections are made up of formal and informal ties. Formal ties are dictated by job titles and roles. Informal ties are generated from chance encounters, various collaborations, or other social connections. These connections can be strong, as when you share a robust personal or professional connection, or weak, as when you are familiar to another person but have generated little professional or social capital.

Beyond the value already established for making the Relational Web the center of your agility shift, there are additional benefits to extending this mind-set and strategy to the entire system. Making this shift:

- **Builds trust:** Strong ties increase the likelihood that members will trust they have the skills and knowledge to get the job done.
- **Improves knowledge transfer and sharing:** Large, diverse networks increase the possibilities for chance encounters, which leads to more knowledge sharing.
- **Increases response time:** You know from your own experience that you are much more likely to respond to a request (or get a response) from a person with whom you have built some

social capital. Strong ties increase the chance that you (or the opportunity you present) will get a rapid response.

- **Fosters engagement:** The more connections you have, the greater your opportunities to make meaning, which leads to greater engagement.

The Center for Creative Leadership (CCL) found that 86 percent of senior executives believe that working across boundaries is important for business success. However, only 7 percent rated their organization's ability to do so as "very effective."[3]

These executives understand that attending to the health of their organization's interconnecting webs is crucial to performance. Members of stagnant networks get stuck in the mud as they reinforce one another's perspectives, drawing only on existing knowledge and becoming increasingly insular. Without regular infusion of new members and perspectives, they may resist the new and disruptive ideas necessary for innovation. The Make Shift Happen practices that follow will help you maximize agility within your current organizational structure while weaving a wider Relational Web to support and sustain your agility shift.

Make Shift Happen

Foster Intraorganizational Connections

Create groups that foster employee camaraderie and make sure everyone feels included and welcome.

Connections that span the functional, departmental, cultural, and physical boundaries *within* your organization lead to greater degrees of knowledge and resource sharing. Some of these encounters happen by chance, and many larger organizations are creating physical spaces to increase these odds. Google's legendary gourmet cafeterias and the campus feel of Apple, Facebook, Microsoft, Zappos, and other companies are designed to make space for such connections.

Even without an unlimited design budget, you can create the physical, virtual, and social space for intraorganizational connections. Leaders at any level of the organization can initiate these connections. However, to support and sustain the agility shift, all must know that they are encouraged and supported at the enterprise level.

Organizations can either implicitly or explicitly discourage ties across boundaries of status or role either through policy or cultural norms. For example, in some formal, hierarchal companies, leaders are asked not to socialize with staff. Organizations that choose to make agility a strategic priority need to reexamine the premise and assumptions of such policies. They need to find ways to protect organizational interests while supporting the development of robust ties throughout the organization.

To shift from agility-impeding cultural norms and interaction-limiting practices, organizations can foster boundary-spanning connections by supporting the following kinds of activities:

- **Interest and affinity groups:** When people gather around shared interests, culture, and/or language, divisions of job title, status, age, and other distinctions slip away. Participation in such gatherings, whether informal and occasional or formal and regularly scheduled, fosters a sense of belonging, safety, and mutual support that may be more elusive within formal networks and project teams. All you need is one or two interested people and an agreement on logistics to start your group. Next, spread the word via high- or low-tech channels to be sure all employees are aware and know they are welcome to join in.

- **Communities of practice:** These communities are intentional and intrinsically self-organized around certain job functions or departments. Regardless of the organizing topic, these communities are spaces within which people can share and experiment with new ideas and best practices, or can come together to troubleshoot and problem solve.

- **Book and journal clubs:** Whether recreational or vocational in nature, such gatherings provide an opportunity for critical reflection and cross-pollination. Rotate the facilitator role each month to avoid burnout and keep the perspectives fresh.

- **Social/intramural groups:** Many a connection has been made on the company volleyball team or square dance outing. One of my clients has a weekly lunchtime knitting group, which was organized by an employee who loves to knit. While these groups and outings are best self-organized, organization-level support can encourage inclusiveness and access for people of diverse ages, backgrounds, and ability levels.

- **Volunteer projects:** Nothing connects people like a shared service project. Umpqua Bank, along with many employers of choice, invites all associates to spend up to forty paid hours each year volunteering, and many employees use this time to volunteer for company-sponsored community projects.

Working within the givens of your organizational resources, make space, information, and, ideally, funds available for those interested in leading or participating in intraorganizational opportunities.

Turn, Turn, Turn (Over Your Membership)

To maximize your Relational Web's potential, seek moderate turnover. This will positively disrupt conformity and comfortable routines without slowing innovation and responsiveness.

Researchers Maxim Sytch and Adam Tatarynowicz studied the patent rates (a key indicator of innovation) of tech firms over a twenty-year time span and discovered that those whose networks had moderate turnover (45 percent over the twenty-year study span) filed almost 20 percent more patents. They also found that too much turnover (70 percent) disrupted knowledge transfer and sharing, as well as the established trust and social capital. Too little turnover likely limited access to fresh knowledge, relationships, ideas, and perspectives.[4]

When it comes to our networks, the lesson is the same one our grandmothers tried to teach us: moderation in all things. This, of course, does not mean that you arbitrarily disrupt teams and networks, but that you look for stretch opportunities for yourself and others. While there is no universal magic turnover number, a good criteria to use is if you are getting a little too comfortable in your role or have stopped learning and growing, it may be time to look for a new opportunity, or to coach a colleague to expand his horizons. Volunteer groups often rotate leadership roles so that no single person is overburdened, and also so more people have a chance to serve and expand their abilities. By seeking such opportunities to turn over your membership, you will reap rewards, along with needed fresh perspectives and resources.

Location, Location, Location

When possible, improve the proximity between members of your Relational Web as you coordinate key collaborators and project teams.

Physical proximity to others in the network counts. In an age where technology provides almost limitless options for connecting, it may be surprising that physical proximity to others within your network can still make a difference. This is one reason that Google, Facebook, Microsoft, and many other companies large and small invest significant funds in their on-site campuses.

It turns out that the secret to success in innovation is the same as it is in real estate: location, location, location. Sytch and Tatarynowicz research also found that those located in the physical core of their networks, while maintaining a moderate rate of turnover, had the highest rate of innovation.[5] Technology can enable communication but it cannot make up for chance encounters in the lunchroom, on the volleyball court, or at parent–teacher night. Such encounters deepen connections and make space for novel combinations of people, ideas, and resources. Proximity of colleagues increases the possibility for knowledge spillover and improves the organization's ability to keep up with emerging trends, developments, and discoveries. Highly distributed organizations can take advantage of these findings by creating space for virtual sharing of informal connections and knowledge. One organization I work with holds virtual potlucks with its internationally distributed team. Relationships are deepened as people show and describe their various regional dishes (and later swap recipes online for all to enjoy).

Structuring for the Agility Shift

J.R. Galbraith, author of a seminal book on organizational design, claimed that "there is no best way to organize."[6] For those making the agility shift, the size, complexity, and unique needs of your business will largely determine which structures, and ways of structuring, enable optimal interactions in your organization. To make the agility shift, you need to know if your organizational structure enables leaders and teams at all levels of your organization to create and sustain a Relational Web; understand the relevancy of their work in relation to the company's mission and goals; and be responsive, resilient, resourceful, and reflective.

No structure can compensate for lack of effective decision making and action, or substitute for a dynamic Relational Web. However, some organizational forms are more likely to enable connections, build relationships, and encourage sharing of knowledge and resources across functional areas. The graphic below shows a continuum of common organizational structures, along with their associated characteristics.

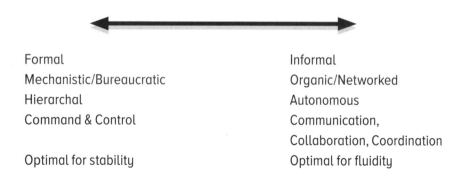

Formal	Informal
Mechanistic/Bureaucratic	Organic/Networked
Hierarchal	Autonomous
Command & Control	Communication, Collaboration, Coordination
Optimal for stability	Optimal for fluidity

For many years the prevailing thinking was that the organizational design should match the complexity of the environment and market within which it operated. Businesses that need to be especially responsive and innovative should be designed with minimal structure and maximum room for the creation of emergent, organic patterns of interactions.

For example, this philosophy drove Zappos to strip all employees of their job titles, design open office space, and create ad hoc project teams.[7] Zappos's success has shown how well a simple structure can work. Minimal structure improves new product development and enhances improvisation capacity. This presents a good case for intentional organizing, using only the most necessary lines of authority and complexity.[8] Such practices enhance the entire Relational Web, making it rich with informal boundary-spanning ties that foster innovation and responsive action.

While the agility shift points toward less formal organizational structure, I caution against an overly prescriptive response, one that jumps on the bandwagon of one extreme or another. Since the dualistic nature of formal and informal structures became common business school fare, the conversation, thinking, and research surrounding them have evolved and matured.[9] Formal structure need not be demonized, as there is evidence that strong informal ties can compensate for impediments created by a formal organizational structure. For example, a fraternity brother who is the head of finance may help you get an expedited answer to a crucial resource question.

Swinging too far in one direction or the other along the formal/informal continuum can also cause an organization to lose its reason for being or its focus. Too much fluidity dilutes the shared purpose, identity, organizational memory, and brand capital, while too much formality can overly constrain the relational ties necessary to get things done. This is especially true for nonroutine occurrences requiring swift decisions and actions, as when an organization must respond to a crisis or new opportunity.

Structuring for agility means balancing the effects of formality and informality. A degree of formalization is necessary to retain identity, while informal structures provide fluidity and responsiveness.[10] Organizations making the agility shift are finding a dynamic middle ground upon which to centralize or create hubs for many key management functions, such as human resources, marketing, and finance. At the same time they are flattening out and networking across other projects and services, such as R&D, sales, and distribution.

When structuring for agility, fluidity and stability are not competing values. A robust, if dynamic, identity—along with structures that support efficient routine operations—creates a culture of engaged and responsive action.

The Make Shift practices that follow offer some guidance on building on the strength of your existing structure(s) to enhance your organizational capacity for agility.

Make Shift Happen

Identify Your Bare Spots

Create opportunities to identify the bare spots in your Relational Web, bridge the gaps, and build mutually beneficial relationships.

Bare spots are not just the vexing patches on your lawn. They exist in almost every organization. For example, let's say the new guy in marketing has an important order to close over the weekend and needs the sales director to sign off on a special contract accommodation. However, the sales director is on vacation, and no one knows how to contact her. These "structural holes" are the relational gaps in your network, and they can impede agility.[11]

While the fire at Ericsson's microchip manufacturer proved a turning point for its cell phone business, the same event had a different outcome at rival Nokia. Nokia not only quickly perceived the urgency of the situation, it was able to work its intra- and interorganizational ties to find alternative suppliers with little disruption in production. The time to identify and close those gaps by weaving an organization-wide Relational Web is not while in the midst of a crisis or opportunity. It is now.

There are numerous ways to identify your bare spots:

• Large companies can employ one of the growing number of network analysis software platforms and/or consulting firms to learn more about the key dynamics of their networks, including the people employees collaborate with most consistently to reach their strategic goals, perform their jobs, and innovate. In addition, this analysis can help you understand the informal ties and social dynamics in which trust, energy, and engagement are fostered and thrive. It is essential that such analysis be conducted from a strength-based perspective, lest it backfire and create a surveillance or punitive culture.

- Smaller organizations, departments, and teams can discover their bare spots through their continuous learning and reflections cycles. The SOAR process of identifying strengths, opportunities, aspirations, and results is an excellent framework for identifying network relationships and gaps, as leaders at all levels commit to new strategic priorities and initiatives. For each new project, action item, and opportunity, create a map and/or database to link needed skills, knowledge, talent, and capacity with individuals and other networks that might have what you need.

- Be generous. Generosity breeds generosity. When people see others in their network actively share and tap their intra- and interorganizational ties, they are much more likely to do the same, especially if they see that generosity is recognized. It is common practice to give employees referral bonuses when they tap their network to help fill a position. While I don't recommend monetary rewards for those who help close network bare spots, regular shout-outs to those who do can reinforce generosity and inspire others to follow suit.

Ask: How's This Working?

Get regular input on how your structure(s) are enabling or impeding your ability to be agile. Ask, "What structural barriers to agility can be lowered or removed? What agility enablers can we amplify?"

Continuous learning and reflection is a recurring theme throughout the stories of agile leaders, teams, and organizations. This extends beyond the lessons learned about the content and intended outcomes of agile collaborations to the structures, processes, and premises that guided (or impeded) effectiveness. Agile organizations are dynamic human systems of interactions. With continuous and intentional reflection, dynamic systems are not trapped in the patterns they create.

Resist the Urge to Formalize

Resist the urge to formalize or create guidelines for processes that include human interactions, creativity, problem solving, customer service, or an opportunity for a novel response.

It is human nature to want to formalize or institutionalize even the most basic of patterns as they emerge. Agile organizations maintain a creative tension between organizational stability (routines) and adaptability (freedom from routines). Agile organizations and their leaders know that too much routine often brings with it inertia and disengagement.[12] Structures and routines that enable clear pathways for communication, collaboration, and coordination, as well as decision making and action, should not have to be re-created at each occurrence. However, too much structure and routine can limit adaptability and the employee engagement crucial for responsive action. If you have ever had the pleasure of interacting with a customer service representative who is obviously following a script, you know what I'm talking about. How much better is it when customer service reps are empowered to engage authentically and immediately, rather than going through a chain of managers to get approval? Less formalization creates better customer service.

Distinguish between processes that enable agility and those that impede it, and formalize only those that are routine and require little variance (e.g., expense report submissions) and/or are necessary for compliance or regulatory reasons.

Agile Systems and Processes

Spanish retailer Zara, founded in 1975, overtook Gap in 2008 as the world's largest clothing retailer. The retailer was able to do so in part by making the agility shift to systems and processes that maximized its ability to spot fashion trends and quickly get new styles in stores.

The hallmark of Zara's success is its ability to collect and interpret real-time data from both the market and in-store sales, communicate these trends through its network, and respond quickly. Data is shared widely with designers, marketing managers, and buyers at the company's headquarters in La Coruña, Galicia, Spain. Not coincidentally, Zara's home office was designed with an open office plan to maximize collaboration, communication, and coordination. Zara now produces as many as ten thousand new designs each year, many in a two-week product development cycle that was previously thought impossible, all while making a commitment to avoid the outsourced, cheap labor and "fast fashion" strategies of many other inexpensive clothing retailers.[13]

At face value, Zara's story appears to counter the agility shift "from information to interactions." Look a little deeper, though, and you will find that the opposite is true. To enable the degree and speed of information it needs, Zara shifted from a structure that looks like a static map of roles and reporting relationships to one that is a dynamic Relational Web for interaction. Such a shift must also include a shift in key organizational dynamics of communication, trust, collaboration, coordination, resources, and knowledge sharing. These dynamics only come to life when the participants in the web have awareness of and access to systems and processes that support and enhance communication, collaboration, coordination, and decision making. The following examples will help guide you in putting these systems and processes into action.

Collaboration: At its most basic, collaboration means to "co-labor," or work together. Today, cloud-based systems and processes that enable collaboration are flooding the market. Before adopting or adapting a system to enhance and expedite collaboration, LaTodd Williams, operational excellence leader and scrum master at Ericsson, recommends that you:

- Assess the aspects of collaboration you want to enable and enhance
- Verify that the technology or tool you are assessing will really help you do that

- Assess whether you have the resources and commitment to train everyone in your network to use and adopt it
- Verify that the prospective technology is compatible with and accessible to your customers and with the outside vendors with whom you collaborate and wish to share documents, data, and access

"It makes no sense to make a big investment in a new tool, only to find out that you are the only ones who can use it," counsels Williams. He also warns against being overly optimistic that any one technology or system will solve all your problems; he suggests that organizations consider assembling a suite of technologies and be prepared to adapt them as collaboration needs and organizational dynamics change.[14] Finally, return to the most essential criteria for collaboration systems and processes and determine whether they improve your awareness of and access to the skills, knowledge, and talent you need to respond effectively to unexpected and unplanned issues and opportunities.

Communication: Whether you are a member of a SWAT team discovering an unexpected obstacle in the midst of a drug raid or a CFO spotting an unexpected drop in revenue, your ability to communicate with others quickly, and to assess the situation, regroup, and respond, are key to your success. SWAT team members may rely on eye contact and hand signals in the heat of the moment, while the CFO may need real-time access to market data, expenses, and other resources. Just as the SWAT team makes sense of an unfolding situation through their interactions with one another, the CFO makes sense of the unfolding picture through interactions with the sales team, customers, and other stakeholders.

In the age of interactions, systems and processes for communication must be as free as possible of barriers, like the red phones in each Umpqua Bank location mentioned earlier. While the red phone may not be appropriate for your business, it can serve as a wonderful metaphor and provocation for you to create several access points from which to gather needed customer insight and connect with your colleagues. Communication is only as valuable as the *community* it fosters and the Relational Web it helps to weave. As you explore and adopt communication systems and processes, stay aligned with your specific needs. It is as essential to have systems and processes in place that foster true communication and dialogue as it is to have those that can quickly and effectively send an all-company memo.

Coordination: From a networking perspective, a single coordinate represents a location in the network. Two or more locations coordinate when they share a dynamic relationship with one another. Flocks of migrating birds and championship sports teams possess an uncanny ability to coordinate in real time, with little or no planning or explicit communication. They have a tacit knowledge of their roles and positions while maintaining an awareness of current activity and shared purpose. They have a shared intention *to* coordinate.

Agile software development teams coordinate each morning in a short stand-up meeting, quickly sharing updates and emerging issues, and use a range of systems and processes to continue coordinating throughout the workday. Agile developers are more focused on creating working software than completing tedious documentation. After the challenging holiday season of 2013, UPS and other shipping companies began working more closely with major retailers to coordinate their resources and better anticipate shipping volume. UPS even began working with individual customers to find packaging that better fits items shipped in order to maximize space in delivery trucks.[15] Effective coordination begins with shared values, is guided by intention, and is facilitated by a commitment to systems and processes that enable effective action.

Decision Making

Beyond decision rights, decision speed is a critical factor for sustained organizational success. Not all decisions are created equal. Some are strategic and have broad implications for the allocation of resources and overall direction of the organization. Others are operational and may only influence how things get done in a particular area or unique instance.

Organizations making the agility shift are doing so because they are operating in increasingly dynamic markets. In this context, the ability to make decisions more quickly than your competitors can provide a distinct advantage. Additionally, decision speed and decision rights are critical to sustaining engagement. The more removed an employee is from critical decision making, the less likely she is to stay engaged and feel empowered to respond to emerging issues and opportunities in the future. This understanding is embedded in and guides agile methodologies in which agile teams, those closest to the issues and opportunities, are empowered to assess, decide, and act in the best interests of the project.

Humans tend to operate under the belief that our decisions are rational and follow a linear and logical process. In reality, the process is messier and more influenced by our emotions and biases than we realize. Recognizing the limitations, management thinker Henry Mintzberg and professor Frances Westley suggest it is time to move past a reliance on "thinking first" and embrace processes that include "seeing first" and "doing first."

"Seeing first" means using insight and experience to discover possible solutions. "Doing first" benefits from trial and error or incremental decision making, and is often used when the situation is novel and confusing, and when things need to be "worked out."[16] Mintzberg and Westley challenge us by saying, "Isn't it time we got past our obsession with planning and programming, and opened the doors more widely to venturing and visioning?"[17]

The agility shift requires a mind-set change with regard to decision making, one that takes place within the Relational Web and is grounded in relevance to shared values, purpose, and bold imagination. The Make Shift Happen practices that follow will help you create systems and processes for more agile collaboration, communication, coordination, and decision making.

Make Shift Happen

Expand Collaboration for Strategic Decision Making

Expand engagement to build the capacity for strategic decision making across the organization.

Engaged employees and stakeholders are much more likely to be agile employees. Many agile organizations are transcending the dualism of centralization and decentralization by including as many employees and stakeholders (customers, suppliers, community members, and others in the ecosystem) in the strategic decision-making processes. This may seem unwieldy, however, it can be accomplished creatively and expediently. I work regularly with leaders throughout organizations to develop strategies that engage the shared values, passion, and talent of the organizational Relational Web while cocreating strategic vision and priorities owned by leaders at all levels of the organization. It is human nature to resist what we didn't have a hand in creating and to embrace that which we co-created. Regular opportunities to engage in such cycles of reflection and action not only strengthen the Relational Web, they expand the entire organization's capacity to innovate and respond effectively to emerging issues and opportunities.

Converge Planning and Action

Create systems and processes that enable planning and action to converge within your Relational Web, and prioritize rapid decision making and action.

Just as there is no one right way to organize for agility, there is no single way to improve decision speed that fits all organizations and instances. More important than how you improve decision speed is that you adopt it as a strategic priority throughout your organization. Leaders at all levels need to know it is a shared value, one they will be recognized and rewarded for enacting. Truly agile organizations are performance organizations, where planning, decision making, and action converge. Understanding the power of converging planning and action drives Zara's competitive advantage and the systems and processes it has established for enhanced collaboration, communication, and coordination, described earlier.

Empower Operational Decision Making

Empower employees to act when they see an opportunity that is aligned with your vision, mission, and values and that helps advance your strategic goals.

If you are not sure which decisions and actions you are empowered to make and which need additional review and approval, you still have room to make the agility shift. The saying goes, "It's better to beg for forgiveness than to ask for permission." Organizations making the agility shift rarely put their employees in the position of begging for forgiveness, because they have already empowered them to make operational decisions. Umpqua Bank gives universal associates permission to go out of their way to make decisions that best serve the customer. New employees are regaled with heroic customer service stories during their orientation to reinforce this permission. Umpqua Bank and others making the agility shift know that many opportunities won't wait for leadership approval or committee review.

Conceiving of your organization as a dynamic system of interactions represents a radical shift in the way most of us were taught to think and act at work. It is a shift from thinking and behaving as if organizations are fixed, immutable entities to intentionally organizing and cocreating new possibilities through each interaction. This shift requires networks, structures, systems, and processes that enable us to easily become aware of and connect with people and resources wherever they are in the organization's Relational Web. It demands practices that prioritize communication, collaboration, and coordination over power, authority, and control. Of course, as you implement these practices, your organization will become more agile, and as your organization becomes more agile, you will see improved communication, collaboration and coordination throughout the system!

The practices described in this chapter are not discrete, one-time projects to implement; rather, they represent a commitment to the intentional and continuous fitness of the system. In the next chapter, we throw the net (or web) even wider to tap the power of the larger business ecosystem for sustained agility and innovation.

CHAPTER SEVEN

Maximizing Agility Within the Ecosystem

When he made plans to fly to Boulder, Colorado, for the annual Champions Retreat for leaders of sustainable businesses, Mightybytes CEO Tim Frick envisioned several days of camaraderie, as well as idea- and resource-sharing. He had not planned on wading knee-deep into mud, but when torrential rains caused unprecedented flooding and damage in the billions that year, that is exactly what he and his fellow B Corp leaders did.[1]

Rather than spending their unstructured time touring area B Corp businesses as they'd originally planned, the leaders rolled up their sleeves (and pant legs) and got to work rebuilding roads and clearing debris from local sustainable businesses. Not only did this network of socially and environmentally conscious business leaders support the community, they all left the conference with stronger ties forged by their collaborative effort. "It was personally rewarding to help Boulder residents stranded in their homes without access to groceries, amenities, and in some cases electricity," reflected Frick, who spent an afternoon rebuilding a washed-out mountain road. "I didn't expect meaningful relationships with business leaders at Method, Plum Organics, and Ben and Jerry's to come out of these efforts as well."[2]

You do not need a flood to recognize the imperative of extending your Relational Web beyond the increasingly arbitrary bounds of your own organization. In fact, organizations that consistently learn, adapt, and innovate depend on the relationships and resources of this web. While it has always existed, it wasn't until James F. Moore introduced the term "business ecosystem" in a perspective-shifting *Harvard Business Review* article some years later that it entered the language and strategy of business more widely.[3]

> This ecosystem includes "intentional communities of economic actors whose individual business activities share in some large measure the fate of the whole community."[4]

In addition to being made up of interdependent entities, the ecosystem includes the local and global communities that participate in the economic and cultural life, educational institutions that develop the workforce and serve as centers of research and innovation, the environment and natural resources, and, of course, the geopolitical, legal, and legislative climate.

"Business ecosystems condense out of the original swirl of capital, customer interest, and talent generated by a new innovation, just as successful species spring from the natural resources of sunlight, water, and soil nutrients," says Moore.[5] Business systems, unlike biological systems, are social and relational, and are made up of larger patterns of interactions and sense making, meaning making, and decision making, as well as intentional (and occasionally unintentional) action.

Shifting from an organizational to an ecosystem mind-set has significant strategic implications. This shift occurred in the technology sector during the 1980s and revolutionized the way computer operating systems were developed and marketed. At the time, major tech players such as IBM and Hewlett-Packard competed largely by developing and deploying proprietary operating systems, creating overwhelming barriers for new companies wanting to enter the field. Bill Joy, master computer architect and cofounder of Sun Microsystems, reflected at the time that the shift occurred with the decision to "change the game...rather than try to win the game as it was currently designed."[6]

To make its products more attractive, Sun Microsystems collaborated with AT&T and gave birth to the open systems movement when they agreed to collaborate to promote "interoperable hardware" based on the open operating system Unix. In the end, AT&T did not win the game, as others soon adopted open source, and were able to do it more cost effectively, but the collaboration set an important shift in motion. Large tech firms started to move from competing solely on proprietary operating systems and began communicating, collaborating, and coordinating within the interdependent ecosystem.

Today, organizations are recognizing that more intentional participation in the ecosystem can greatly expand their agility capacity. It is easy to understand the dynamics of the business ecosystem by considering what happens each time Apple releases a new iPhone and/or updates its operating system. Not only are all of Apple's direct suppliers engaged and affected, but so are all the companies that design and sell accessories and apps, as well as *their* suppliers, customers, and stakeholders.

Value of a Healthy Ecosystem

In a healthy ecosystem, new ideas and opportunities thrive, to the mutual benefit of many members in the system, not just a small group within it. Those making the agility shift are enjoying the benefits of intentionally cocreating a healthy ecosystem to enhance their capacity for innovation and responsiveness, as well as local and global citizenship.

Innovation

All members of a healthy ecosystem benefit from the exchange of ideas and talent. Those making the agility shift expect themselves and other members of the ecosystem to practice continuous learning and innovation.[7] One such mutually beneficial joint venture was fostered by the College of Nanoscale Science, at SUNY Polytechnic founded in 2004, and its Center of Excellence in Nanoelectronics. Through this collaboration, faculty, students, and engineers from 250 corporate partners work together on a wide range of innovative projects, some of which are then spun off as new business ventures facilitated by the SUNY business school. Based on its initial success, several leading semiconductor manufacturers, including IBM and Intel, invested $4.4 billion to develop advanced chip technologies at the newly created center.[8]

Leaders in other sectors have strategized to tap the power, and contribute to the health of the ecosystem, including investor Chris Nyren, who founded Educelerate. This consortium brings together educators who have specific challenges and opportunities with entrepreneurs and investors interested in creating innovative solutions. Nyren intentionally chose to focus his attention on the Midwest and Southwest, often overlooked as a vibrant network of cocreative opportunity in the education ecosystem.[9]

Social entrepreneurs also play a significant role in cocreating a healthy ecosystem for the benefit of all members. The missions of social entrepreneurship ventures are centered on innovations that benefit not only (or even primarily) the business stakeholders, but society as a whole. For example, the Global Social Benefit Institute (GSBI), based at Santa Clara University's Center for Science, Technology, and Society, fosters a healthy ecosystem by matching social entrepreneurs with Silicon Valley mentors who help the entrepreneurs identify growth opportunities and resources while refining their business models.[10]

You don't have to be a multinational corporation, large educational institution, or nonprofit to benefit from the cross-pollination of ideas and resources in the ecosystem. Many start-ups and sole practitioners are enjoying the energy, community, and inspiration available in coworking and incubator spaces such as Serendipity Labs in Rye, New York, Workspring in Chicago, and WeWork Labs in New York and San Francisco. Accessible to those working with minimal resources, such spaces are thriving around the country and provide both strategic and accidental opportunities to incubate and cross-pollinate ideas, share resources, and vastly expand each inhabitant's Relational Web.

Many businesses today are thriving by expanding the creative capacity of the Relational Web throughout the ecosystem through open innovation or by seeking ideas and collaborators well beyond the walls of their organization. Well known examples include IBM, Philips, and Microsoft. Companies that are not household names are also working within and leveraging the power of the ecosystem, such as, Enablon, a French company that produces web and mobile device sustainability, health and safety software. By collaborating with every client Enablon develops a solution that both meets each client's needs and works within the ecosystem of their clients and of other hardware, software, and database providers. Other companies have built their entire business model to rely on the ecosystem for a stream of innovative ideas and to solve pressing problems, including:

- **Quirky**, a crowdsourced invention company that taps its 100,000-plus community members for new product ideas. The ideas with the highest number of votes are put into production.[11]
- **Threadless**, a Chicago-based apparel company that began in a studio apartment when its founders decided to hold an online T-shirt design contest. It now uses crowdsourcing for all of its product designs.[12]
- **GitHub**, an open source software resource that allows developers to access, create, improve on, and share code, as well as find projects and collaborators. GitHub has grown to be the world's largest open source community.[13]
- **Foldit**, an online puzzle game that taps the online gaming community to help understand complex protein configurations. In 2010, 57,000 FoldIt players were credited with providing useful results that matched or outperformed algorithmically computed solutions.[14]

These are just a few examples of agile organizations across sectors and of all sizes that reach beyond their org chart for expanded capacity to innovate. Attending to the health of the ecosystem also enables organizations to more quickly and effectively tap resources when the unexpected and unplanned hit.

Local and Global Citizenship

To be an effective member of a healthy ecosystem, you need to co-create value for all members, including local and global communities. This, of course, is in everyone's interest. For example, on a local level, if arts and education organizations are thriving, it is certainly easier to recruit and retain talent who want to live in such communities. From the small digital media company Mightybytes to the growing regional bank Umpqua and the global enterprises of UPS and Ericsson, active participation in the ecosystem is key to their success.

Mightybytes is a leader in local and national sustainability efforts, including the B Corp movement, which promotes sustainable business practices, and Climate Ride, which raises funds for climate change awareness and action through charitable endurance events.

B Corps across the globe—including Patagonia, Ben & Jerry's, Method Products, Dansko, Plum Organics, and Etsy, to name just a few—use the power of business to solve social and environmental problems. With the business and natural ecosystem in mind, the B Impact Assessment grades each B Corp on criteria of environmental impact, transparent governance, relationships with workers, and corporate citizenship within its community. Like many B Corps, Mightybytes finds value within the B Corp ecosystem as fellow B Corps become both clients and vendors, mentors and mentees, all striving for the same goal of shared prosperity.

Umpqua Bank takes another approach to cocreating a healthy ecosystem across its entire system of more than four hundred locations. Through the bank's Connect Volunteer Network, employees are paid for up to forty hours per year to volunteer for local school and community development projects. In 2014, 67 percent of employees participated, racking up more than 53,000 hours of volunteer time.[15]

On an even broader scale, UPS has joined others with robust logistics resources and expertise to support disaster preparedness efforts and deliver urgently needed supplies to stricken areas.[16] Also on a global scale, Ericsson has embraced its agility shift and is now a leader in creating global access to electricity through its Community Power Solution and Millennium Villages Project, which it developed in partnership with Swedish green site solution specialist Flex-enclosure as part of a portfolio of innovative services and products. This new initiative draws on largely renewable energy sources to bring power to remote villages in Africa.[17]

Agile organizations like these execute projects and initiatives within and for the health of the entire ecosystem of interdependent entities, organizations, and stakeholders and, of course, benefit in return by being able to do business in and with the same healthy ecosystem. Every organization, no matter its size, must include the ecosystem in its agility shift strategy if it expects to quickly access knowledge, innovative thinking, and resources.

These benefits do not happen by accident, of course. Just as a natural ecosystem falls out of balance when one species dies out, leaving others without serious predators to keep its population in check, organizations that strategically acquire or merge with all of their significant competitors can have unchecked control of resources and pricing, which is not only unhealthy for consumers but diminishes the robust interorganizational ties that lead to innovation. These strategies may lead to short-term gains but eventually destroy the diverse ecosystem necessary for sustained success.

The values embedded in the companies involved in the B Corp movement and those embracing the triple bottom line of people, planet, and profits help ensure that the business ecosystem is healthy for *all* its inhabitants. The Make Shift Happen practices that follow offer specific ways you and your organization can begin to realize the value of extending your Relational Web throughout the ecosystem you inhabit.

Make Shift Happen

Map Your Ecosystem

Discover who shares your ecosystem in order to become a better participant.

Before you can be an effective participant in your ecosystem, you must first become aware that it exists and know who and what is living there with you. The best way to do this is to begin by mapping your ecosystem. You may choose to begin this process in collaboration with a few organizational leaders, however it is best to include as many stakeholders as possible in order to ensure you have included all of the side streets, not just the major highways, that connect the inhabitants of your ecosystem.

No organization is too small to benefit from understanding and appreciating its place in the ecosystem and the extent of its Relational Web. Understanding who you cohabitate with and the nature of the relationships allows you to be intentional about how you participate in these relationships, as well as to identify gaps and opportunities to expand or realign your network.

Ecosystems can be mapped from the perspective of a specific product or service, work group, organization, or entire industry segment. To start, identify the perspective, unit, or level of the business you want to map. There is no one right way to create your map—the important thing is that it inspires you to think well beyond the boundaries of your organization and to become a more active and productive participant in it. Using Moore's original concept of the business ecosystem as a starting place, I ask my clients to make lists of some of the ecosystem inhabitants they want to include on their maps. These often include:[18]

Core business:

- Key contributors
- Distribution channels
- Essential resources
- Product and service vendors

Extended enterprise:

- Customers
- Customers' customers
- Supplemental suppliers
- Suppliers of our suppliers

Other inhabitants, stakeholders, and influencers:

- Dream clients and prospects
- Competitors
- Educational institutions and think tanks
- Industry organizations and networking groups
- Investors
- Government and regulatory agencies
- Community organizations

Once you have named the inhabitants of your ecosystem, identify the nature of the relational ties within and between its members. This includes coding these relationships in terms of their relationship to your organization and to one another: C=Customer, S=Supplier, I=Influencer, SP=Strategic Partner, TL=Thought Leader, CMP=Competitor, IN=Innovator, E=Educator. Note that many ties will have multiple designations. You may also want to designate which ties are "strong" (it's a consistent and mutually beneficial connection), which are "weak" (the connection is inconsistent and/ or only beneficial to one party), and which hold potential but are not fully developed.

Here are some of the connections we made in a recent ecosystem mapping session at Mightybytes:

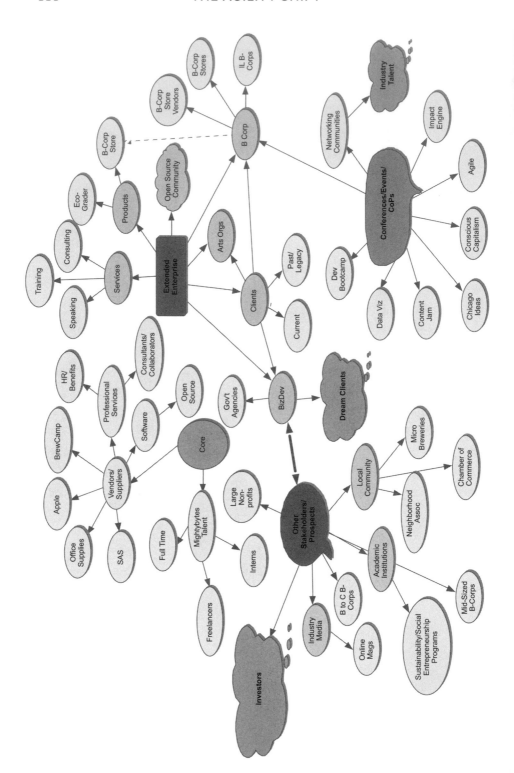

Use Your Map

Learn how to use your map to get directions to agility-enhancing relationships and resources.

It doesn't help to have a map if you don't use it. One of the best ways to begin to leverage the power of your place in the ecosystem is to ask inhabitants on your map for directions. Use the key dynamics of the agility shift as a guide, and consider the following questions as you get started on your way:

• **Relevant:** Are we in relationship with others who are best aligned with our mission and values? If yes, how might we build a strategic alliance to be more effective in achieving our mission? If not, whom else might we seek out?

• **Responsive:** In what ways does our place in the ecosystem enable us to be responsive to client needs, as well as to the unexpected and unplanned? How can we expand our relationships within the ecosystem to become more responsive?

• **Resilient:** When the unexpected occurs, how do we tap our relationships within the ecosystem to regroup, recover, reorient, and reenergize? Are there other relationships we might foster that will help us to be more resilient?

• **Resourceful:** How do we engage with the ecosystem to expand our capacity to innovate and make effective use of available resources? With whom might we build stronger ties to expand our capacity to innovate and serve our clients?

• **Reflective:** How do we currently participate in our ecosystem for continuous learning? How might we be more intentional in the ways we engage with the ecosystem for learning and reflection?

These questions are only a starting point, and are intended to help you expand your role and participation in the ecosystem to maximize your capacity to be agile. Once you have mapped your ecosystem and begun to ask it for directions, your answers will guide you in cocreating a more agile ecosystem for mutual benefit.

You may then use your map to ask for directions on additional strategic issues, for example, changing your perspective to that of one of your competitors and exploring how that organization is engaging in the ecosystem. You can also ask for directions with a specific strategic focus, by asking yourself how innovation happens in your ecosystem and whether the current inhabitants have the knowledge and resources to incubate and develop new products and services.

- How do your customers participate in the ecosystem?
- Are they getting maximum benefit from the relationships and resources available to them?
- How might you help them and other inhabitants benefit from available opportunities while keeping your own strategic interests in mind?

Questions like these will help you identify new markets for your existing products and services, as well as opportunities to innovate in response to unmet needs.

Weave Your Interorganizational Web

With your map as a guide, initiate idea- and resource-sharing opportunities for mutual benefit.

The capacity for innovation and responsiveness often live in the relationships between organizations. It is in relationship that novel ideas collide, collaborative learning occurs, resources are combined, and new ventures flourish. Organizations with robust interorganizational ties have greater capacity to innovate and respond to the unexpected.[18]

Your original ecosystem map will reflect your current reality to the degree you are currently aware of it. In the previous chapter, you were prompted to identify the bare spots in your *intra*organizational network. As you pan out to view your organization as it coexists within the broader ecosystem, you have a similar opportunity to identify the bare spots in your relationships to and with other inhabitants.

The team at Mightybytes wanted to leave the rough draft of their ecosystem map posted in the conference room for several days, featuring groupings of sticky notes of all sizes and colors connected by spaghetti strings of whiteboard marker lines. As team members wandered in and out of the conference room and pondered the map during meetings and on lunch breaks, more connections and ideas began to emerge. Within a week, CEO Tim Frick e-mailed me with a long list of ideas the group had generated, completely unprompted, for ways to build relationships, gain visibility, and offer more resources, services, and products for mutual benefit. I challenge you to co-create such a map, leave it in your shared space, and *not* start generating your own list of ecosystem-boosting ideas. You won't be able to stop yourself!

Make It Easy for Others to Weave into Your Web

Do transparent by sharing those aspects of your map that will help others find their way to your opportunities and resources.

If your goal is to build interorganizational ties for collaboration and innovation, potential partners need to be able to weave their way into your Relational Web. In 2012, IBM launched its Supplier Connection to help small businesses connect with large corporations that might be in need of their products and services and to tap into the more than $150 billion in annual supply chain spending from its flagship partners, including UPS.[19]

To ensure that your potential partners can find their way to you, you must regularly invite the kinds of neighbors and collaborators with whom you would like to cohabitate and whose ideas and resources you would like to share. It helps to view your organization or entity from the outside and ask yourself:

- If I were a customer, how would I share my frustration, compliment, or a suggestion?
- If I were an educator or thought leader, how would I connect with

innovators in the organization to propose investment in/sponsorship of a new idea?

- If I were a supplier with a more sustainable or cost-effective product or service, how would I get the attention of the right person or department?

- If I were a community stakeholder wanting to partner with the organization to improve the quality of life, education, and culture in our area, how would I start building a relationship with decision makers?

- If I were another local, national, or international business or government agency interested in building a strategic partnership, how and where would I start the conversation?

- If I were an industry association interested in booking one of the organization's leaders for the next international conference, how would I go about it?

Once you have answered these questions from the perspective of the inhabitants in your ecosystem, you need to create a way to evaluate the potential value of these relationships. In some cases, the value is intrinsic to the relationship itself and has a relatively low cost (time taken to attend a networking event, conference, or guest lecture at a local university), so needs little scrutiny. In other cases—such as when you are creating an internship program with a local high school or college, or are creating RFPs for an open innovation strategy—the investment, infrastructure, and allocation of resources may be substantial. This type of investment requires clearly defined evaluation criteria that include analysis of cost benefit, time, talent, and resource allocation, together with associated training needs.

Find, Co-create, Invest, and Participate in Incubation Centers

Support the centers of learning and innovation that nourish and sustain your ecosystem.

Your ecosystem is only as healthy as the new ideas it generates, incubates, refines, and implements. All participants have a shared stake in a healthy ecosystem. Organizations that are thriving engage in at least one of these ecosystem-sustaining activities:

• **Finding** existing centers for innovation and exploration. These centers may exist informally or formally within area colleges or universities, nonprofits, or community/government agencies, or may be found in professional or industry association special interest groups or professional development networks (PDNs). You will locate these centers of innovation and idea sharing as you map your ecosystem; if you find that those that exist do not serve your current needs, try starting one (see next point).

• **Cocreating** a think tank, skunk works, or community of practice for experimenting, piloting, and community building. These endeavors provide low-risk, low-cost opportunities to innovate while building the capacity and resources to mobilize quickly when opportunities arise. Everyone in your team, department, or organization knows at least a few colleagues outside the organization who are committed to continuous learning and innovation. Invite them to your offices or even a local coffee shop to talk about the trends and burning issues you are seeing. It is possible to create a community of practice even in highly proprietary environments by taking the time to establish some shared agreements and ground rules. Be sure to include educators and thought leaders in your community, together with others who can provoke your thinking and perspectives.

• **Investing** your time and resources to support and sustain centers of incubation and innovation. This may mean offering your conference room or virtual meeting space, volunteering to organize and convene the sessions for a set period of time, or investing modest or significant financial resources to seed innovation projects. The entire ecosystem can benefit from such investment, through the educational, economic, social, and environmental opportunities nurtured there.

• **Participating** in the hubs and communities that are most aligned with your interests and values. More than any other resource, participation sustains the value and quality of these spaces for incubation and innovation. Participation is more than just showing up; it means showing up bearing gifts. These gifts may come in the form of a provocative new journal article, a suggestion for a collaborative project, an introduction of a new strategic partner, or an offer to share your expertise in an emerging technology, to name just a few. Your commitment to participating and sharing gifts will inspire others to reach into their own goody bags and do the same. Generosity begets generosity. Why not be the first to set the gift giving in motion?

Each of these practices will greatly expand your ecosystem and link you to ideas, resources and talent you likely don't even know you need!

By becoming aware of and embracing your role as cocreator and participant in a dynamic ecosystem, you will not only be making an agility shift in mind-set and strategy, you will expand your capacity to respond to the unexpected and you will weave an increasingly resilient and resourceful web to sustain your success. In the next section, we turn our attention to the people practices that will enable you to develop, recruit, reinforce, recognize, and retain your agile workforce.

Part Two Summary

In the chapters in part 2, you have been invited to view agility from the vantage point of leaders and teams, as well as from that of the entire organization and the wider business ecosystem. The boundaries between these levels of the system are largely artificial but, for our purposes, it is helpful to isolate them in order to identify specific approaches that you can implement within your span of influence. Regardless of your role in your organization, it is essential that you keep each of these vantage points in mind and regularly shift between them. Consider, for example, whether your agility shift strategy or practice enhances agility for leaders but actually makes things more complicated for teams. Or think about whether your strategy is taking full advantage of the resources available within the wider Relational Web and ecosystem. The shift at each of these levels of the system is one of both mind-set and practice. The mind-set shift includes appreciating that, while you may not have power *over* your entire organization, or even your peers, you do have power *to* become more effective and agile by adopting and adapting many of the practices described here. In part 3, you will learn how to share responsibility for sustaining your agility shift with innovative learning and development strategies and people practices.

PART THREE

to Work

CHAPTER EIGHT

Shifting to Agile Learning and Development

When Anne Schwartz took a job as a package driver at UPS she had no way of knowing that she was embarking on a career that would last more than twenty-seven years and take her through four promotions and six moves throughout the United States and Asia to her current role as vice president of global leadership and talent. Today she is responsible for the global training and leadership development strategy for the largest package delivery company in the world. She has gone from being responsible for the safe delivery of several hundred parcels each day to supporting the success of more than 400,000 employees in 220 countries.

> "You are here today, then your job is over there tomorrow and that's how quick we actually move."
>
> —Anne Schwartz[1]

Schwartz's journey is a testament to the potential unleashed when a driven (pardon the pun) employee takes advantage of and creates her own opportunities within a system designed to develop agility and leadership. The two go hand in hand. Each new role gave Schwartz the opportunity to stretch her capacity, develop and discover new competencies, and gain confidence in performing and delivering results in increasingly high-stakes arenas. UPS's commitment to developing and promoting top talent from within also gave her the opportunity and necessity to think on her feet, work with the available resources, and continue to innovate.

Describing the UPS strategy, Schwartz explained, "We continue to rotate and take on new roles and responsibilities, sometimes with relocations, and generally learn from the bottom up. We have been around over one hundred years, and our founding fathers felt very strongly about taking the people that we have, giving them new broader experiences, and pushing them beyond their capabilities to expand the business and their personal capability."[2]

Despite the reality of today's rapidly changing global business environment, most business schools and training approaches are designed to prepare leaders to be effective in stable environments. Unlike the intentional learning and career development approach I highlight here, they assume knowledge and skills learned today will be applicable to tomorrow's conditions. While a growing number of schools and training programs include courses on agility and improvisation, the vast numbers of formal training programs are still based on the underlying premise of stability. This translates into learning and development that focuses on the aspects of organizational dynamics they can control, which is why so much time is spent on planning and analysis.

As I have emphasized throughout, the agility shift does not mean throwing your plans or data analysis out the window; instead, it means giving at least equal attention and resources to the practices that expand your capacity to be effective when things don't go as planned. It also means shifting to a mind-set of learning as continuous and social, rather than as a solo event.

In this chapter you will discover key aspects of the learning and development mind-set and strategy shift you and your organization must make to become more effective performing in today's unpredictable and complex reality.

Agile Learning for Learning Agility

To begin the necessary mind-set and practice shift for preparing and sustaining a learning-agile workforce, we need to challenge some basic assumptions about learning and development. This starts by asking some seemingly obvious questions, such as: "What is learning for?" and "When has it occurred?" Asking and answering these questions with agility in mind will lay the foundation for approaches to learning and development that will help you and your organization be more effective in the midst of changing contexts.

What Is Learning For?

Your pre-VUCA mind-set answer (if you answered the question at all) was likely fairly straightforward: to develop new skills and knowledge, to improve business results, to get things done, to improve customer satisfaction, and so on. These are still valid answers in a VUCA world. However, they are not sufficient to shift your mind-set and improve agility.

The purpose of learning in agile organizations is not just basic skill and knowledge development, it is also to improve and expand the Relational Web and to enhance individual and team effectiveness in changing conditions. This type of learning includes the ability to make optimal use of available resources, effectively frame problems and opportunities, make expedient decisions for action, and expand the agility capacity of your leaders, teams, and entire organization.

Each of these reasons for learning is less linked to content or planning and analysis skills than it is to expanded agility competence, capacity, and confidence. When we shift our understanding of learning, we also shift the learning and development opportunities we seek and develop.

What Are We Learning and When Has It Occurred?

Effective performance in changing, uncertain conditions calls for us to expand the types of knowledge we value. Agile performance depends on more than operational knowledge and skills (know how) and understanding (know what) that can be shared or transferred from one person to the next. It requires that we expand and increase awareness of relational, embodied, reflective, and contextual knowledge:

- *Relational knowledge* lives within our relationships to other people, ideas, material resources, and experiences and does not easily pass from person to person. For example, you can tell me all about your favorite Uncle Bill, which will give me knowledge *about* him, but I would only gain relational knowledge by engaging with him directly.

- *Embodied knowledge* is the intuitive, tacit understanding and awareness that lives in our bodies. For embodied knowledge, our bodies are both the site of learning and the source of knowledge.

- *Reflective knowledge* is distinct from the reflective process described elsewhere in this book. It is gained through direct experience, as individuals and groups interact with one another, learning and cocreating cultural and ethical norms.[3]

- *Contextual knowledge* is understanding and appreciation of the conditions and dynamics of a specific situation, challenge, or opportunity. These may include cultural, environmental, power and authority, stakeholder, economic, geopolitical, and social dynamics.

These types of knowledge can only be fully gained through direct experience and cannot be given to others like holiday gifts. Knowledge that cannot be stored in a database is at least as important for agility as knowledge that can be codified. In each of the agility shift stories told throughout this book, the organizations were successful, in part, due to the relational, embodied, and contextual knowledge that enabled them to quickly coordinate and collaborate with others in response to their challenge or opportunity. Agile organizations value and intentionally inquire about not just *what* knowledge they are acquiring, but what *types* of knowledge.

This expanded appreciation of knowledge runs counter to the behaviorist perspective that most of us were trained to use to assess learning and performance. From a behaviorist point of view, the definition of learning was simple: learning has occurred when we see a change in behavior. It's true that, when assessing agility, you want to see an increase in effective communication, collaboration, and coordination. However, if you only look for agile behavior, you will miss evidence of the other types of learning that underlie the change in behavior. Before a change in behavior can be observed, other types of learning have to take place, and other types of knowledge must be acquired. We can see evidence of these types of learning and knowledge acquisition when:

- A mind-set is expanded or shifted
- A way of thinking or being changes
- Decision-making processes are impacted
- Self-awareness and awareness of others and group dynamics increase
- There is more trust among collaborators and organizational leaders
- Networks expand and/or strengthen
- Past experience is applied in a new and unfamiliar situation

Each of these representations of new learning reflects a 180-degree shift from what Paulo Freire termed "the banking model of education," where new information is simply deposited in the brain of the passive learner to be withdrawn at predictable intervals.[4] Learning and development for agility requires whole-person engagement to prepare the learner to be effective in unpredictable, ambiguous, unfamiliar, and often changing contexts.

Whole-person engagement includes the very real possibility that those who are learning will themselves be changed in some way by the process. Change is risky. It can threaten our fundamental beliefs about ourselves, our competence, and even the way we are seen by others. No wonder people resist it! All learning and development strategies for agility must include a commitment to creating a safe environment for learning to occur.

It is also important to look for the crucial components of self-awareness, awareness of others and the context, as well as attitudes and demeanors that enable agile performance. Many of these attitudes and demeanors have been highlighted in past chapters, including mindfulness and attitudes of realistic optimism, anxious confidence, curiosity, and perseverance. You don't need a survey, however, to know how people are feeling about their work; just look around and you will see for yourself! The agility shift is a performance shift, and agile performance is dependent on sustaining attitudes and demeanors, along with opportunities for continuous learning and development.

From Competence-Based Learning to Agile Performance

In my first career, I worked as a professional stage manager in the theater for both well-resourced and not-so-well-resourced regional theaters and later as a director and producer of small, often experimental, productions. In the world of the performing arts, competence is expected, but it won't get you the role. It may not even get you an audition or interview. All that matters is your performance, in the moment, under the lights, and often in the midst of the unexpected and/or unfamiliar.

Organizations making the agility shift need to think beyond competence-based learning and create conditions and opportunities for all of their players to perform at their best. This does not mean overlooking competence; it means thinking of competence as the pathway to performance, when competence meets confidence and capacity in action.

In the table on page 134, each of the agility shift dynamics is translated into competence statements. I then show the primary types of knowledge and skills each competence requires. These competence statements and types of knowledge will help you identify learning experiences to help develop the agility shift competence. Of course, competence is only valuable if it serves as a pathway to performance. You will then find performance indicators for each competence in the right column, to help you determine when learning has occurred. Each indicator can (and should) be assessed at the level of the individual leader, team, and entire organization.

Performance indicators include both process indicator, such as employee engagement and satisfaction, and indicators of business impact, such as revenue, profitability, market share, customer loyalty, and earnings per share. These indicators are crucial for sustaining and growing your business and keeping your stakeholders happy. I share each performance indicator as an example in the hope that you will refine and build on those that are most relevant to the needs of your leaders, teams, and organization.

Performance indicators are directly linked to the real reason to care about the agility shift: the meaning, purpose, and happiness people experience when they are making a difference doing something important. This is also what will ultimately sustain your commitment to agility practices over the long haul.

As you review the learning and development framework, don't be fooled by the nice, neat table. The types of knowledge, skills, practices, and performance indicators cut across each of the five agility shift dynamics and the Relational Web. I have highlighted those most strongly correlated to specific competences. In doing so, I want to emphasize that the related knowledge, skills, and practices, as well as performance indicators, are by no means mutually exclusive. Separating them in the table is intended to help you target the areas you are in greatest need of developing. For example, your Relational Web may be healthy and growing, but if your Responsiveness is dismal, you and your organization have an excellent starting point for your learning and development strategy.

The Agility Shift Learning and Development Framework

Competence	Types of Knowledge	Skills and Practices	Performance Indicators

Relational Web: The ability to identify, co-create, interact with, and sustain a dynamic core of relationships for sense and meaning making, as well as idea and resource sharing	— Relational
	— Contextual
		— Inter– and intrapersonal
		— Networking
		— Social media/networking systems and processes
		— Ecosystem mapping
			— Employee engagement in internal and external networks
			— Employee satisfaction
			— Size and diversity of social networks
			— New business development
			— Customer satisfaction
			— Vendor/strategic partner relationships
			— Ecosystem health:
			  ○ Innovation
			  ○ Education
			  ○ Talent acquisition

Relevant: Ability to clarify values and use them to inform organizational purpose, decision making, and action	— Reflective — Contextual — Business trends and innovations	— Communication — Leadership — Critical thinking, problem and opportunity framing — Values clarification — Scanning and filtering: ability to make meaning and sense in the midst of complexity (intentional rapid cycling)	— Employee engagement and retention — Brand integrity and reputation — Competitive advantage via innovation and responsiveness — Market share

Responsive: The ability to respond quickly and effectively to the unexpected and unplanned, as well as to emerging opportunities	— Embodied
	— Contextual
		— Improvisation
		— Communication, collaboration, and coordination
		— Decision making
		— Mindfulness
			— Response effectiveness:
			  ○ Situation/opportunity resolution
			  ○ Positively responds to the opportunity
			  ○ Makes optimal use of available resources
			  ○ Expands the capacity of the individuals and entities involved

Competency			
Resilient: Ability to regroup, reorganize, and renew in the midst of unpredictable and changing conditions and contexts	— Relational — Contextual	— Game finding: recognizing and influencing patterns — Learning agility — Continuous learning — Cognitive reappraisal — Rest and renewal practices	— Timeliness (both literal and relative) — Customer satisfaction (both internal and external) — Responsiveness is a brand differentiator — Effective decision making and action in alignment with team and organizational goals — Capacity to change course as new information/knowledge and conditions warrant — Sustained or renewed energy and engagement in current projects, initiatives, and creative explorations — Timeliness of recovery following a disruption — Dynamic engagement with purpose — Positive brand identity and associations
Resourceful: Ability to use, and improvise with, all available resources, including human, technical, and environmental	— Operational — Resource awareness	— Improvisation — Identify and play within the givens — Rapid prototyping — Comfort with uncertainty and change — Curiosity	— New product development/patents (number, quality, profitability) — Productivity — Effective use of Relational Web for both challenges and opportunities
Reflective: Ability to learn in and from experience, and apply that learning in new and changing contexts.	— Embodied — Contextual	— Learning agility — Reflecting in and on action	— Continuous improvement and innovation — Speed of project implementation and product development

Shifting Your Learning and Development Strategies

By now it should be clear that agility does not happen by chance. Those who are consistently agile make intentional shifts in their mind-set and strategies. In learning and development terms, this means making a shift from an approach that only values learning outcomes to one that also values learning processes.

Before you can improve these processes to maximize performance, you must first know how you are currently learning or, in fact, if you are learning at all. For example, despite growing evidence that 70 to 90 percent of workplace learning is informal, many learning and development strategies heavily favor formal (designed) learning.[6] Making matters worse, some studies show actual learning transfer from formal learning back to the workplace hovers between a dismal 10 and 34 percent.[7] Leaders, teams, and organizations interested in maximizing learning in general, and learning agility in particular, need to pay attention to how they and their successful colleagues are actually learning and shift their strategies.

All learning starts with experience.[8] Studies of learning-agile executives show that the most valuable learning experiences happen on the job. New and unfamiliar situations in the workplace challenge you to think on your feet and draw on prior experience. The knowledge and skills gained can help inform your gut feelings and intuition.[9] Learning that happens on the job, or at least with immediate relevance to current challenges and opportunities, is learning that sticks. It sticks because it was learned experientially and in a context that is meaningful.

In other words, not all learning opportunities are created equal. Research shows that, in addition to experience-based learning, the learning opportunities that have the most significant impact on learning agility are those that are "emotional, require risk-taking, and have real-life consequences."[10]

In addition to shifting *how* we learn, the agility shift has significant implications for *who* is responsible for learning. If learning starts with experience, it follows that the person or people most responsible for the learning are those who are having the experiences and those who are accountable for their individual, team, and organizational success. Successful leaders, as well as those who want to become successful leaders, regularly seek out new learning and development opportunities. A leader must identify which areas need development and select those learning experiences that will improve performance, rather than wait for someone else to identify and respond to their learning needs.

Crossing the Formal/Informal Learning Divide

With the agility shift in mind, learning and development professionals, and all who learn, must fluidly cross a once-sacred divide. This is the divide between formal (training classes and coursework, whether on site or online) and informal learning (learning that happens on or related to the job). Such either–or approaches invite compartmentalization of strategies and roles rather than integration and shared ownership.

Workplace learners can become more effective in transferring learning from formal settings to new and changing contexts, while learning and development professionals can design their courses to maximize relevance and transfer by using a range of new strategies. Salman Khan popularized, though didn't invent, the notion of the flipped classroom, in which much of the content is delivered outside the formal classroom or learning environment, often via prerecorded video lectures and tutorials. The classroom is then used for experimentation with new knowledge and development and for practice of new skills.[11] Many workplace learning professionals are now using flipped learning strategies to maximize the impact of their formal or on-site time with their learners.

As the gap between learner and learning professional shrinks, the roles of both begin to shift. The learning professional is relied on less as a content designer and facilitator and more as a guide or knowledge manager, who points self-directed learners to learning resources, such as documents, blogs, wikis, communities, recordings, sound or video bytes, people, job aids, as well as to formal courses. The learner's role also shifts from passive recipient to active seeker of new knowledge and learning experiences.

Make Shift Happen—For Agile Learners

I have broken this longer series of Make Shift Happen practices into two segments. The first set of practices is written with you, in the role of intentional, responsible learner, in mind. They provide a wide range of learning activities across the formal and informal continuum that you, as a responsible learner, can seek out or develop to make the shift from agility competence to agile performance.

Stretch Yourself

Seek out stretch experiences to expand your ability to learn and adapt in the midst of change.

If you ask successful executives or entrepreneurs about the learning experiences that enabled them to develop the competence, capacity, and confidence to achieve at the highest level, they will tell you about the times when they were thrown into a new role, with little preparation, and had to draw on all available resources and learn along the way. These are the stretch experiences and roles that were pivotal to Anne Schwartz's success, whose story opened this chapter, and they can be for you and your colleagues, as well. Those who seek out and/or are given such opportunities will become learning agile much more quickly than in any other way. Here are a few such stretch experiences:

- Assignments that challenge you to work outside your comfort zone
- New leadership roles, especially those that expand the scope of your prior experience

- Living and working in a new culture
- Mentoring and coaching to help you seek out new learning opportunities and mine those experiences for lessons learned

An added benefit of stretch assignments and promote-from-within strategies is the opportunity to develop business literacy and expand your Relational Web and awareness of available resources.

Cross-Train

Just as athletes cross-train in a variety of sports, you can become more agile by cross-training in a variety of roles in your organization or profession.

One of the best ways to get and stay fit, regardless of your sport, is cross-training. For Umpqua Bank, and many others like it, cross-training is the key to organizational fitness, agility, and the ability to be responsive to customer needs. All Umpqua branches (stores) are staffed with universal associates who can open an account for you, help you with your 401K, refinance your mortgage, or get you logged into your e-mail at their free Internet café.

Agile leaders understand that an urgent customer need, a supply chain crisis, or an opportunity to innovate will not wait for a carefully crafted proposal to be developed and run up the chain of command for approval. Understanding the limitations of this now outdated leadership mind-set is what drives Umpqua Bank's approach to recruiting and its strategy of continuous learning and development. Umpqua knows that it cannot afford to lose a customer because he is waiting for someone with the proper training in the particular product or service to become available. By cross-training all employees as "universal associates" Umpqua ensures that all who interact with customers have the necessary skills, knowledge, talent, and motivation to be responsive. In addition, the organization empowers and inspires associates with examples and organizational stories that give them encouragement and permission to go the extra mile at each opportunity.

Similarly, UPS has expanded its capacity for agility through promoting talent from within to ensure that its leaders truly understand how business gets done and how to support those working on the front lines. Ericsson is likewise expanding its capacity for agility by launching new centers for excellence to teach the lessons of agile project management, collaboration, communication, and coordination throughout the organization.

Cross-training does not mean having a team or organization full of "jacks-of-all-trades, masters of none." In fact, for the communication, collaboration, and coordination necessary for agility, it is much more valuable to have a team of "generalizing specialists," or "jack-of-all-trades, master of a few."[12] Such colleagues understand, at least at a high level, the systems, processes, challenges, and opportunities in each dimension of the entire initiative, project, or new product development cycle, but are expert in just a few. Generalizing specialists are able to effectively communicate and coordinate with their colleagues by sharing relevant information along the way.

In my first career as a professional stage manager, in addition to managing most facets of the day-to-day production process, my role was to constantly scan each rehearsal and production meeting for new developments that might affect others (for example, when the director asked the costume designer for a character to make an entrance wearing a two-foot-tall headdress. This development had immediate implications for the set and lighting designers, who had to accommodate and light the actor as she made her stately entrance). Without a basic understanding of the entire process, and others' roles, it is impossible to know which new developments are relevant and worth acting upon.

Make the Most of Formal Training Experiences

Set learning goals and reflect on and apply your learning to increase your chances of being able to draw on your new skills and knowledge when it matters most.

Just because most workplace learning happens outside the classroom does not mean formal learning is without value. In fact, successful executives report that classes, workshops, and other training opportunities are particularly useful when they are timely and relevant to current projects, issues, and opportunities.[13] Relevance and linking new learning to prior experience are key brain-friendly principles of adult learning. Certainly, instructional designers and facilitators must share responsibility for making the learning meaningful, memorable, and motivating (3M's criteria for successful e-learning learning).[14] However, those who make the most of these experiences greatly improve their success by taking a few moments before, during, and after the learning experience to intentionally make it relevant:

- Think about your current work or life challenges and identify skills, knowledge, and capacities that would help you be more effective.
- Prior to participating in formal learning experiences, identify your personal learning goals (these may differ from those described in the course materials).
- Share your learning and development goals with a colleague or supervisor before you participate in the formal learning experience.
- Keep a learning log to make note of key insights and particularly relevant lessons, as well as questions and topics for future exploration.
- Within a few days of the learning experience, meet with your colleague or supervisor and share your learning as well as the progress you made toward your learning goals, and discuss how you can implement/experiment with your new learning.
- If possible, create an opportunity to share your learning more broadly with colleagues via a brown bag lunch, company newsletter, or blog post.
- At the first opportunity, experiment with putting your new learning into practice and reflect on your results.
- Repeat.

If you haven't noticed, there is a recurring theme in each of these best practices: intentionality and a willingness to shift your mind-set and behavior.

Make Shift Happen—For Agile Learning and Development Professionals

This next set of practices is specifically designed for those whose role includes helping others become more agile. This, of course, includes learning and development professionals, however the material is relevant for everyone who shares responsibility for sustaining an agile organization. In addition to sustaining your team and organizational agility, there is another great reason to share the responsibility for learning: research shows that the best way to make your new learning stick is to share it with others.[15]

Prototype New Learning Strategies

Improve responsiveness to learning and development needs by rapidly prototyping and testing learning strategies.

Typically, workplace learning strategies are developed using the ADDIE approach, where the requirements are gathered and analyzed up front, the learning program is developed and designed, then it is implemented and evaluated. If this sounds familiar, it is because it is based on the same waterfall approach that many software developers have abandoned. Just as software developers discovered, many learning professionals are finding that this process is not very effective for rapidly changing needs, not to mention that it simply takes too long to go through the entire cycle. Once the cycle is completed, more often than not the designers discover at the evaluation stage that there are new needs or conditions that were not known at the start of the process, and these must be incorporated. An alternative approach to the limitations of this cumbersome process is to shift to rapid prototyping, or SAM (successive approximation model), developed by Michael Allen.[16]

Originally conceived for designers of e-learning, rapid prototyping for agile learning means quickly identifying the learning issue or opportunity, the type of knowledge or skills needed, and the optimal learning experience to develop the knowledge and skills. Rather than rolling out the learning strategy after a long, drawn-out process, prospective learners are invited into the process early to test, provide feedback, and, of course, learn. This feedback, along with any available evidence of the learning experience's impact on the learners' performance back on the job, is then used to drive the next iteration.

Agile learning and development for learning agility are essential for changing contexts. If those who are developing the learning strategies are unable to quickly recognize and respond to learning needs in their organizations, they have little chance of enabling agility in others.

Create Whole-Person Learning Experiences

Develop and provide learning experiences that engage the whole person and whole brain to maximize learning agility.

Leaders, teams, and the human systems we call organizations need to be able to rapidly make sense and meaning of what is happening so they can respond effectively. Whether they are being agile in a boardroom, on an improv stage, or as they storm a suspected drug operation, those who are able to continue processing new information while staying creative under stress will tell you that their skills didn't develop by chance.

The competence, capacity, and confidence to perform effectively in uncertain, changing contexts is developed over time, with practice and in contexts with incrementally increasing stakes. Agility, and more specifically, learning agility, also requires learning that engages the whole person and the whole brain. These strategies are:

- **Embodied:** They invite people to get out of their seats (as they are able) and move in ways that are most aligned with the learning opportunity.
- **Emotional:** They involve some level of risks and/or stakes.
- **Complex:** They include learning challenges in which there is no one right way to be effective; situations have unknowable variables that defy prescriptive answers and, ideally, require collaboration, communication, and coordination for success.

Over more than thirty years working with improvisers in the theater and helping businesspeople develop their improvisation competence, capacity, and confidence, as well as studying those who improvise for a living in high-stakes contexts, I discovered some consistent themes. For novice improvisers in the theater, the biggest fear is often that they will freeze on stage, not be able to think of anything to say, and look like complete idiots. Though the stakes may be higher, SWAT team and film crew members and businesspeople share the same initial fear.

One of the biggest surprises for those learning to improvise is that the best improvisers are often not those who are naturally funny in a stand-up comedy sense. In fact, stand-up comedians often make horrible improvisers because they lack the ability (and interest) to be team players. The best suggestions for developing agile performances include:

- **Incrementally increase the level of risk.** Start with low-risk games and exercises where everyone plays and no one is in the spotlight. We know the brain's capacity to engage the neocortex, the site of complex thinking, greatly diminished during stress. When the reptilian brain takes over, we are reduced to an organism capable of three responses: fight, freeze, or flight. In these low-risk games, improvisers increase their capacity for such stress as they learn to play in the dynamic present moment, develop essential skills like saying, "yes, and..." to new ideas and discoveries, make their partners look good, and make continuous discoveries.[17]

Whether in a formal learning setting or through workplace assignments, you can seek out low-stakes opportunities to increase your comfort and build your confidence as well. This could involve finding opportunities outside of work in volunteer settings that allow you to take on new roles or it could mean taking classes that let you practice in a simulated space. This is one of the reasons Toastmasters International, the amateur public speaking association, is so popular. At weekly meetings, members have many opportunities to practice a wide range of impromptu and planned speaking in front of a supportive audience. With these examples as inspiration, you, and/or the learners you are designing and facilitating for, will experience success in low-risk experiences, and can then incrementally increase the stakes and complexity.

- **Habituate scanning and filtering.** Improvisers quickly learn to scan the environment and identify their givens for the *who, what,* and *where* and begin playing within them. SWAT teams and Navy SEALs train to make OODA (observe, orient, decide, and act) a habit.[18] To be effective on these playing fields (it is no coincidence that battle fields are called "theaters"), the players must habitually scan and filter all of the incoming data (visual, auditory, embodied, extra-rational, cultural, cognitive, and more). You can use similar strategies for any workplace context by developing scenarios and inviting your "players" to draw givens from separate who, what, and where envelopes to get the action rolling. As the players develop their capacity, you can increase complexity by adding unexpected twists, such as "You have just received word that your top competitor is getting a similar product to market three months before yours is set to launch."

At the organizational level, leaders can develop scanning and filtering habits as they review new developments, trends, and ecosystem shifts for relevance. For example, in the winter of 2014, UPS leaders shifted their attention to its ecosystem and used their capacity to observe, orient, decide, and act to track falling gas prices, which they viewed as a possible indicator of increased holiday spending and, by extension, higher shipping volume.[19]

- **Be an improv coach.** When an improviser freezes on stage, most often it is because she has left the present moment and has lost her ability to scan and filter and be responsive to her new discoveries. Improv teachers are masters at side coaching (whispering gentle prompts from the sidelines that do not interrupt the action) to help novice improvisers develop these habits and return to the present moment. Prompts such as "Notice your environment," "Make some new discoveries about the object you are holding," "Stay with that feeling a bit longer," or "Heighten and explore this new discovery" help players maintain a dynamic relationship to the moment and habituate continuous learning in increasingly complex contexts. Depending on the context, side coaching can also be done via text messaging, video chat, or mobile apps. Before long, these prompts become internalized, and improvisers are able to coach themselves to unfreeze, scan, filter, and be creative in the present moment.

Work Out

Hold regular workout sessions to help your colleagues stay in "agile shape," develop, and practice new competencies in low-stakes settings.

No sports team would consider taking the field with even the most talented individuals without weeks or months of rigorous workouts and team practices. Similarly, improvisers, while they don't technically "rehearse" because there is nothing to "re-hear" in improvisation, do regularly get together to work out, play improv games, hone their skills, and build team capacity to collaborate, communicate, and coordinate in the dynamic present. Organizational psychologist Philip Mirvis calls this kind of "rehearsed spontaneity" an essential aspect of team and organizational success and a critical success factor of "anxious confidence."[20]

SWAT and other special ops teams also regularly rehearse by working out a wide range of complex scenarios and conditions.[21] These scenarios can be designed with increasing degrees of risk and stakes. In introducing the concept of agile project management and scrums, Jeff Sutherland, cocreator of the Scrum software development process, likes to unleash teams on several rounds or "sprints" to create a paper airplane that will meet some very basic initial requirements (givens). Success in the exercise demands effective collaboration, communication, and coordination, along with continuous learning throughout. Create your own version of this exercise or design another sprint challenge opportunity to help your colleagues develop their own abilities through direct experience.

Facilitate with the Whole Person and Brain in Mind

In facilitating whole-person/whole-brain learning experiences to improve agility, it is important to design and facilitate with two critical success factors in mind:

1. **Allow ample time for the embodied activity:** All too often, facilitators rush the experiential aspect of learning because of the mistaken belief that the real learning happens in the debrief. In fact, important whole-person/whole-brain learning is happening *during* the experience

itself. The brain and body are becoming more aware of what happens to our bodies and brains under stress and experimenting with strategies to moderate them. New neural connections and pathways are being formed and strengthened, new habits are being practiced, and even (perhaps especially) new self-concepts are emerging. All of this takes time.

2. **Facilitate reflection with learning agility in mind:** If all learning starts with experience, facilitators need to first spend some time helping learners attune to *what* they were experiencing. Questions such as, "What did you notice going on in your body?" and "How did your breathing or heart rate change?" are helpful to prompt such awareness. Next, probe for the relational dynamics that were in play: "How did you engage your Relational Web? Interact with others? Communicate? What ways did people take on leadership roles? What behaviors were most effective?" As a facilitator, you can also help learners develop habits of cognitive reappraisal by asking, "What story did you tell yourself about what was happening?" or "What other versions of the story might have led to alternative choices?" Finally, prompt learners to reflect on ways they drew on skills, knowledge, and demeanors developed in other settings (whether consciously or not) and what lessons they learned that they will want to experiment with at the next opportunity.

With learning agility as a priority, such strategies can easily be woven into most formal learning experiences. Even the most technical and operational learning can be approached with an understanding that the skills being developed will very likely be used, at least occasionally, in a nonroutine context. Preparing learners to be effective in such contexts is the most important charge of today's learning and development professional.

Use the Power of Information to Change Behavior

Provide timely, actionable feedback to help your learners make the necessary mind-set and performance shifts in a changing context.

In addition to loving stories, metaphors, and direct experience, the brain loves immediate feedback. Improvisers, like many performers, consider the audience a fellow player whom they monitor for feedback as closely as they do those sharing the stage. Engagement (or lack of it), delight, offense, and the entire spectrum of emotion are felt, interpreted, and often responded to by those playing in the dynamic present.

Agile developers give and receive feedback in their daily stand-up meetings; Umpqua universal associates reconnect and recalibrate in their morning motivational moments; and UPS drivers receive feedback each morning and throughout the workday through multiple high-touch and high-tech channels. Sometimes the most effective way to shift behavior is with a live coach observing and providing real-time feedback and support on a ride-along. UPS also provides drivers with a dashboard of comparative information to let them know how they are currently doing in relation to critical metrics of their own past performance and that of other drivers. Even the best-intentioned drivers had trouble improving until they had specific feedback that helped them focus on behaviors they needed to change to improve performance. For example, when a driver knows how much time her vehicle is left in idle, or in reverse (when accidents are more likely), as compared with other drivers, she becomes more motivated to lower that number.[22]

How does this feedback translate to the bottom line? In addition to improving safety, fuel economy, environmental impact, and customer satisfaction indicators, feedback impacts behavior change and, ultimately, company profits. Jack Levis, UPS senior director of process management, shared how: "If we can reduce one mile per driver per day in the United States alone, that's worth up to $50 million to the bottom line at the end of the year."[23] You do not need to be a global organization with a significant budget to tap the power of information and deliver real-time feedback to your workforce. You also don't need sophisticated technology to provide timely, actionable feedback. You do need an understanding of its value and a commitment to using your available resources to deliver it.

Employ Action Learning for Agile Success

Take advantage of your collaborative business practices as part of your overall learning and development strategy.

We have seen that all learning starts from experience. In addition learning that sticks is relevant, timely, and involves emotional engagement and, ideally, a bit of risk. Several of the agility shift strategies described throughout this book, include these essential dynamics because they call for learning in action. Collaborative strategies, such as SOAR and the ecosystem mapping practices that Mightybytes employs, not only engage the entire organization in cocreating a positive future, but are themselves action-learning opportunities. Action learning is learning that happens in the midst of action with the intention of creating positive change. As a wide cross-section of the company gathers to build on strengths and imagine an ideal future, they are also building their agility competencies, capacity, and confidence, as well as their collaboration, communication, and coordination skills. In addition, they are able to identify gaps between their current competencies and capacity, and can collaborate to close that gap by tapping their available resources.

Create Learning Networks and Communities

Use curiosity and shared needs as your guide and convene a community of practice for continuous learning, for resource and idea sharing, and to expand and strengthen your Relational Web.

Creating and sustaining learning networks, learning communities, and communities of practice is essential to sustaining the agility shift.[24] The hallmark of the most successful learning communities is their minimal structure and intrinsic motivation for participation. Value is created because people are motivated to share new learning and best practices without coercion or requirement. These communities have famously emerged to respond to common needs, such as detailing repair issues not found in the Xerox copier service manual or supplying the information new faculty must have to adjust to their roles and successfully negotiate their way through the tenure and promotion process.[25] There is no prescription for forming a community of practice or a learning community other than it be intrinsically motivated (rather than coerced or required) and sustained by the active participation of its members. You just need to make the decision and act. For example, post an on-site or online notice of the focus of your first meeting (e.g., "To discuss latest developments in technology in our field") and then make time during your first session to generate new questions and topics. Utilize these forums for continued idea and resource sharing.

Learning happens everywhere. The question is, what and how are you learning and is it enhancing or impeding your agility shift? Leaders, teams, and organizations who are serious about making the agility shift and realizing its benefits and results share responsibility for learning at all levels of the system and across roles and job functions. In the next chapter you will learn how to sustain your agility shift with best practices for recruiting for agility and for retaining, recognizing, and reinforcing it for business performance.

CHAPTER NINE

Recruiting, Reinforcing, Recognizing, and Retaining Your Agile Talent

Every organization wants to hire top performers and, of course, help them deliver top performances day in and day out. Organizations making the agility shift are not only looking for people with a track record of delivering great results, they are looking for people who can do so when things don't go as planned, or in response to an unexpected opportunity. The challenge is that you can't determine whether someone can perform effectively under pressure from a résumé. To become adept at making that assessment, you must learn from those whose livelihood depends on their ability to find people who can literally perform effectively without a script: improvisational theater directors and producers.

> Just because you can hit a tennis ball, doesn't mean you can win a game.

One of the first things I discovered when auditioning actors for roles that required them to improvise was that there are many talented actors who are great at following a script but are horrible improvisers.

There are also tennis players who play like Wimbledon champions when their opponent is the immovable backboard, but who have trouble scoring a single point against a real-life opponent in a fast-paced, unpredictable game.

The same, of course, is true for organizational performances. There are those who excel at a specific job function and thrive with clear direction and routine operations, and others who thrive in contexts that are continuously changing and provide daily opportunities for new learning and innovation. With the Make Shift Happen practices outlined in the previous chapter, you can (and must) help your *current* workforce develop their agility competencies, capacity, and confidence. However, when it comes to recruiting *new* talent, it only makes sense to hire those who you know will thrive in your agile organization.

Throughout the book I have discussed organizations as dynamic human systems that make the agility shift by expanding their Relational Web both within and beyond their walls. These organizations intentionally and continuously build their competence, capacity, and confidence in each of the five dynamics of agility. Keeping this perspective, this chapter is about the people practices that are necessary to help you sustain the agility shift. Of course, recruiting is only the starting point. There are actually four key quadrants for putting agility to work:

- Recruiting
- Reinforcing
- Recognizing
- Retaining

Many of these practices traditionally fall under the purview of the human resources department, however, for organizations making the agility shift, they should be shared (at best) and understood and appreciated (at least) by leaders throughout the organization.

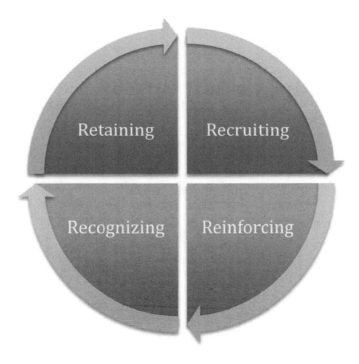

Recruiting

Before you can determine whether prospective agile talent may be the right fit for your organization, you must attract these candidates. The good news is that organizations that are agile generally have reputations for being great places to work. Umpqua Bank prides itself on making the "Fortune 100 Best Companies to Work For" list year after year, not only because it elevates the brand in the minds of customers, but because it makes finding top talent much easier.

Though he is talking about agile developers, Eric Winquist, CEO of Jama Software, shares a common theme among those recruiting for agility in any organization: "The tricky part isn't necessarily about where to find developers, it's about how to identify the agile 'mindset.' There are some technical skills that are necessary— how to run a scrum [an agile software development team], for instance—but for the most part, we're looking for a personality profile; people who are curious, problem-solvers, very collaborative. Those soft skills along with great communication skills are what we want."[1]

In addition to seeking these particular skills, agile organizations recruit for people with attitudes and demeanors that are more likely to be effective in changing conditions. There is a growing body of research that shows that people with high self-esteem coupled with high trust in coworkers perform more effectively under pressure in team collaborations, and those who are "emotionally hardy" tend to have a high tolerance for ambiguity and higher "boiling point" in the midst of complexity.[2]

Google's head of human relations, Laszlo Bock, is not just looking for the emotionally hardy, he recruits those he calls "smart creatives." These are "people with a healthy mix of technical skills, business expertise, and creativity." Bock and other Google staffers who routinely review résumés and sit in on interviews are looking for the person who is "innately curious, [has a] will to learn, and has emergent leadership skills."[3] This is great news for the often-maligned liberal arts graduate. Google, along with many of the businesses and industries I have polled over the years, values critical and creative thinking, communication, leadership, and autonomy over a narrow set of technical skills. Each of the examples of agile leaders, teams, and organizations highlighted here confirms this: the ability to communicate, collaborate, and coordinate is essential to agile success. The challenge is how to identify and recruit those candidates.

Organizations with a strong Relational Web are engaging the power of their networks to find such talent (and reduce recruiting costs). UPS is part of a growing trend of companies that are tapping their Relational Web and ecosystem to recruit top talent via social media with impressive results. In 2009, UPS hired nineteen employees through social media. The strategy worked so well that the company continued to build on its success, and in 2013, UPS recruited 24,475 employees using social media. The cost savings are equally impressive. Within a decade UPS's advertising cost per hire dropped from $500–$1,500 to less than $27.[4]

Once you get qualified candidates in the door, there are three ways to assess their fit and ability to be effective in changing contexts:

(1) direct observation, (2) collaborative inquiry (commonly known as interviewing), and (3) play.

To assess an individual's agility performance, in the best of all worlds, you and/or your hiring managers want to give candidates an opportunity to show you their skills, knowledge, and demeanor in a variety of ways and contexts. The Make Shift Happen practices below are intended to help you recruit the most agile workforce, while setting your prospective agile player up for success.

Make Shift Happen

Observe

Pay attention to the way candidates interact with the environment and others during first encounters.

Seeing agility in action is, of course, the best indicator of competence, capacity, and confidence, and, ultimately, performance. One of the best ways to observe a potential candidate in action is to offer an internship or trial employment period where you and your candidate can collaborate in your organization's natural habitat. Internships are not always possible or practical for either the organization, or the candidate, in which case you must make creative use of some of the more traditional aspects of the recruiting and interviewing process to determine agility competence and capacity.

The recruiting and interviewing process is already stressful for even the best candidates. From the time the candidate arrives, you have an opportunity to see how she functions when the stakes are high and in the midst of the unknown. This includes observing (or getting feedback about) how the new prospect engages informally, from her first encounter with the receptionist to casual interactions with others she meets along the way, and even noting her level of engagement with your corporate magazine or annual report in your lobby. Some of my clients like to take people through the office kitchen and offer them coffee or tea, in part to put the candidate at ease, but also to get a sense of how she interacts with the environment and others. These early informal observations can offer clues about her degree of curiosity, social intelligence, and more. Once everyone is settled for the initial conversation, much can be learned from observing body language, by noting emotional engagement and attitudes, and from the actual content of the conversation.

While I do not advocate being overly choreographed in the initial stages of recruiting, some interviewers have found it useful to observe how their prospects respond to interruptions and changes of plans (e.g., letting the candidate know that the person who was initially going to conduct the interview is not available, or shifting the schedule or settings during the first encounter). Notice whether changes and new information are welcomed as "gifts" or irritants. These may be early clues to a person's ability to be effective when things don't go as planned.

Conduct a Collaborative Inquiry

Partner with your candidate to explore current and past experiences that required agility.

The second-best way to assess a candidate's potential for agile performance is to conduct a collaborative inquiry into his past behavior, as well as to engage him as a thinking partner in discussing current or past scenarios in the organization and probing for his ideas. Unlike the standard stock market warning, when it comes to agility, past (and current) performance *is* quite often a predictor of future success. A collaborative inquiry is qualitatively different from a traditional interview, or even a behavioral interview, for which candidates are likely to arrive with well-rehearsed answers. The inquiry is collaborative and conversational because both you and the candidate are looking for new insights from the experiences you are reflecting on. While I am not a fan of scripts, in the Agile Recruiting Table on page 158 I share several sample scenarios and behavioral questions linked to each of the agility shift dynamics to get you started. There is no magic in any specific question, as often the most interesting insights into behavior and mind-set come from the quality of the conversation itself.

Look and Listen for Agility Competencies

Pay attention to evidence of agility-enabling skills, knowledge and behaviors.

In addition to the competencies articulated in the table, look for evidence of the three agility-enabling competencies of communication, collaboration, and coordination. Evidence of these should be embedded into the stories, examples, and insights you discuss during your observation and inquiry:

Communication: The ability to discern relevant information, developments, patterns, and trends and share them effectively with others who need to know.

Collaboration: The ability to work effectively with diverse others to co-create and/or implement ideas.

Coordination: The ability to synchronize efforts with others whose work you depend upon, and who depend upon your work.

Follow-up questions are a wonderful chance to join in the collaborative inquiry with your candidate. These questions can range from familiar prompts, such as "Tell me more about that" when you hear something particularly interesting or want to probe for more evidence about specifics of the three enabling competencies of communication, collaboration, and coordination. For example:

- "How did you/would you communicate with other stakeholders during that situation?"
- "How did you/would you be sure you were drawing on all of your team's resources throughout that process?"
- "How did you ensure that your colleagues involved in that situation were coordinating their efforts?"

Such questions are intended to prompt new insight and to help you surface behavioral examples, and also to let you see how your candidate thinks, reflects, and learns in action.

Recruiting for Agility

Competence	Sample Conversation Topics/Scenarios and Questions	Listen and Look for Agile Performance Indicators via
Relational Web: The ability to identify, co-create, interact with, and sustain a dynamic core of relationships for sense and meaning making, as well as idea and resource sharing	If we were to hold an open house for prospective customers, and to increase our visibility in the community with key stakeholders: • Whom would you invite? • What networks would you tap? • What other strategies or relationships would you draw on to ensure our success? [Note: Question could be modified to focus on new product and service development or other priorities.] **Behavioral:** Tell me about a new venture in which you needed to tap resources beyond your immediate network. How did you go about finding and engaging the right people?	Listen for: • A wide and diverse range of people, interests, and networks • Specific ideas Look for: • Level of emotional engagement and generativity
Relevant: Ability to clarify values and use them to inform organizational purpose, decision making and action	**Sample scenario:** Our company has built its reputation on innovation and being on trend; at the same time, we have aggressive financial goals. We are exploring an opportunity to partner with an organization that has a much more traditional brand, but that could help us generate significant new revenue. How might we go about making this decision? **Behavioral:** Can you talk about an experience in which your values or priorities were challenged and you had to make a quick decision? Can you tell me how you worked through it?	Listen for: • Values clarification process, creative thinking, and ability to make decisions amidst competing priorities Look for: • Self-confidence while being open to creative ways to move forward

Competency	Questions	What to observe
Responsive: The ability to respond quickly and effectively to the unexpected and unplanned, as well as to emerging opportunities	**Sample scenario:** Frequently in our project work we encounter unexpected issues and opportunities. For example, just this past week we had a team discover that the client wanted X rather than Y (fill in the blank), but still needed us to deliver on time. How would you respond? **Behavioral:** Tell me about a time when you went into a situation thinking it was one thing and quickly discovered it was something else entirely? **Alternative:** Can you tell me about a time when you were thrown into a new role without any preparation?	Listen for: • Ability to think creatively under pressure, focus on customer needs, and tap (perhaps probe for) available resources Look for: • Evidence of drawing on prior experience • Demeanor when the unexpected occurs • Ability to reframe goals and discover opportunities in the unexpected
Resilient: Ability to regroup, reorganize, and renew in the midst of unpredictable and changing conditions and contexts	**Sample scenario:** When we started this company, we experienced X disruption or Y disappointment/ setback (fill in with a specific). How would you have handled it if you had been in Z role? **Behavioral:** Can you tell me about a time when you experienced a significant disruption or disappointment?	Look and listen for: • Strategies and emotional demeanor/attitude for regrouping; how was the candidate able to reframe the situation and move forward?
Resourceful: Ability to use, and improvise with, all available resources, including human, technical, and environmental	**Sample scenario:** See the playful prototyping exercise on page 161 **Behavioral:** Can you tell me about an experience when you had to be effective with limited resources?	Listen for (and give permission to share): • A range of personal and business examples. Look for: • Creative use of resources, attitude of "realistic optimism"
Reflective: Ability to learn in and from experience, and apply that learning in new and changing contexts	**Sample scenario:** In our work we regularly reflect on how things are going and what we learned. What kinds of questions should we be asking ourselves to maximize our learning? **Behavioral:** Can you tell me about a significant experience you have had that changed you? How did you go about learning from that experience?	Listen for: • How the candidate prefers to learn, initiative she takes in reflecting on experiences, learning, and reflection habits Look for: • Varied strategies, use of mentors and others within the Relational Web, curiosity, humility

Play

Create opportunities for candidates to play with your current team members so that your group has direct experience of how it might feel to collaborate, communicate, and coordinate with them.

Even better than talking about or observing candidates outside of their natural habitat is giving them a chance to play in settings that replicate some of the key dynamics of the work they will be doing, even if metaphorically. No matter the size of your organization, you can draw lessons from large, highly customer-focused businesses, like Harrah's Casinos, which conduct interviews like auditions. At Harrah's, for example, groups of thirty to forty candidates are invited to participate in a series of interactive exercises and games, which quickly reveal their ability to perform under pressure.[5] Such strategies are particularly effective in recruiting for roles that require candidates to think on their feet in complex, sometimes stressful situations, and keep their cool while creating a positive customer experience. Alternatively, you can invite prospects to join in a playful scrum or prototyping experience, like the paper airplane exercise mentioned in chapter 8. Below I describe two ways you can invite your candidates to play with you:

- **The agility audition:** This is best begun with a series of low-risk games that are framed only as "warm-up" activities. I have included a few sample games in Appendix B, and more on my website: pamela-meyer.com. It is best to have enough people participating that candidates don't feel as though the spotlight is entirely on them, and include a mix of other candidates as well as current employees. You are not looking for perfection, or improvisational comedic brilliance, but rather at how the players interact with one another, how they deal with inevitable snafus, disconnects, and "mistakes" (I put this in quotes because there are no mistakes in improv, only opportunities).

After your warm-up games, be sure to take the time to reflect on the experience with the candidates to get a sense of their level of presence, embodied awareness, and ability to learn in the midst of a changing context. You may then choose to move into some simple scenario play, by passing around envelopes or hats labeled "Who," "What," and

"Where." Teams of three to five players draw one "given" from each envelope and are invited to use them to begin playing. Inevitably, the random combinations (nuns, at their high school reunion, on the moon?) will provide stretch opportunities in which you will get to see how players make discoveries, build on or block one another's ideas, solve problems, explore possibilities, set one another up for success, and play in the dynamic present moment.

- **Playful prototyping:** Whether or not your organization uses agile methodologies, rapid prototyping is a wonderful way to help people develop their agility competencies and to assess their ability to be effective in a highly collaborative and complex situation with a specific goal in mind. Create a simple, physical, timed challenge, such as building a suspension bridge out of pipe cleaners, solving a puzzle, coming up with a new twist on an old product, or writing a tagline and jingle for an everyday object. In a team, or in several teams of three to seven people, set them loose on their creative collaboration in three to five short, timed sprints (of no longer than three minutes apiece). At the end of each interval, ask the teams to reflect on how they are working together, what they are learning, and what they want to change in the next interval.

The value of playing during the recruiting process is not only to see your candidates in action and observe the ways they are creative and collaborative under pressure, but to give members of your team a sense of how it feels to play *with* them. As with the "agility audition," and just as you would debrief an individual sprint or scrum, at the conclusion of your playful scrum, gather the players together and ask a few reflective questions, such as:

- What were you aware of as you were playing?
- What team dynamics were most helpful in moving the project forward?
- What lessons did you learn that informed the way you collaborated during each iteration and/or that could guide your work going forward?

This guided conversation will provide you with additional insight into candidates' capacity for self- and process reflection, and the degree to which they adopt an attitude of inquiry. Early on, you will get a sense of whether an individual is more concerned about making himself look good than supporting team/project success.

Depending on the size of your organization, resources, or immediate circumstances, it may not be possible for you to include these kinds of experiential activities in the recruiting process. You may find it more manageable to include such opportunities in your onboarding process as a means for your new players to build their Relational Web within the organization and become part of your culture. Mightybytes invites each new hire to choose a beer to brew and to serve as the "brewmeister" during his first month on the job. This regular Friday afternoon ritual is not only a great way for new teammates to learn about one of the passions of many members of the organization, it lets employees collaborate and co-create with new colleagues in a relaxed atmosphere.

Reinforcing

In the previous chapter, I detailed several strategies for shifting from approaching learning as an event to thinking of it as a process that involves continuous learning and reflection. All of the organizations profiled here are making such a shift and are incorporating a number of strategies that not only align with agility shift best practices but that *reinforce* agile performance as it happens. These approaches are embedded in and help build the Relational Web of the organization, while helping leaders, teams, and entire organizations build positive habits in ways the brain actually likes to learn.

Part of this shift is being led by organizations that are moving away from the dreaded quarterly or annual performance evaluation toward more frequent, qualitative conversations.[6] The reason for this is (at least) twofold. For one thing, these quantitative formal assessments do not yield the hoped-for results; second, they are a horrible way to support agile performance, which, by definition, is situational, and not something that can wait to be discussed until the next review meeting in nine months. Debbie Cohen, vice president of human resources at Mozilla, says traditional performance management is an outdated concept. "The entire conversation and mind-set needs to change," says Cohen. To work at the top of their talent and to reinforce agile performance, employees need continuous feedback, not a once-a-year snapshot.[7] By the time annual reviews roll around, the progress, accomplishments, and opportunity for constructive feedback are old news, if they are remembered at all. To support agility, you can reinforce agile performance as it happens guided by the Make Shift Happen practices below.

Make Shift Happen

Make It Social

Create social spaces for positive feedback that reinforce the performance (behaviors, attitude, demeanor, and results) you wish to sustain.

Effective strategies range from high to low tech. UPS's Telematics and ORION systems provide real-time feedback on performance, while managers serve as coaches to keep the conversation relational and developmental. Mozilla has adopted a reinforcement strategy of social performance management (SPM) and uses the platform work.com as one way to provide continuous feedback and to shift to a more agile mind-set.

You don't need to be a global organization with generous infrastructure investments, or to invest in or design a whole new platform, to shift to a social reinforcement and recognition strategy. In fact, sophisticated technology can sometimes distract from the actual human system and the development processes they are designed to support. Several of my clients have created forums for social feedback using existing platforms, such as LinkedIn or Google groups or the bulletin board in the lunchroom.

Social strategies for reinforcing agile performance align with the social nature of the brain and enhance the networks that make up the individual, team, and organizational Relational Web. Because the brain is also wired to protect itself from threat, it is essential that the feedback provided in the social spaces is positive and strength based, reflecting progress toward agreed-upon goals and specific incidents of agile performance. This kind of public feedback is not only motivational, it is also one of the most important forms of recognition, because it is situational and given in a relational context. The space for developmental conversations and constructive feedback is always one-on-one and offline.

Make It a Conversation

Create time and space for quality conversations that reinforce the values and behavior necessary to sustain the agility shift.

The shift away from formal, yearly performance evaluations is a shift *toward* performance conversations. Neuroscientist David Rock helps make the case for shifting to a more dynamic, relational approach to performance with scientific evidence. He and his colleagues at the NeuroLeadership Institute found that only 41 percent of feedback results in performance improvement.[8] With new understanding about how the brain likes to learn, and how it is wired to protect itself from perceived threat, Rock promotes replacing performance evaluations with "quality conversations." One of the reasons for the dismal results of most feedback is that the brain is trained to perceive such feedback as negative and goes into defensive mode. Rock has identified five social situations that activate strong response via the acronym SCARF: status, certainty, autonomy (control), relatedness (belonging, shared goals), and fairness. Because the brain is wired to scan the environment for social threats, when any of these are concerns, the opportunity for learning and change, let alone meaning making and creativity, come to a screeching halt.

Shifting agile performance from an evaluative process to a conversational one can avoid this shutdown and lead to new insight and growth for all participants in the conversation. Rock's research supports what anyone who works with adult learners has known for years—optimal conditions for growth include a healthy balance of support and challenge. Using Rock's criteria, set up conditions for a quality conversation:

- **Share a "growth mind-set."** Both, or all, participants enter with the intention to learn, reflect, and grow.

- **Minimize threat.** We know that as soon as the brain perceives threat, its capacity to make complex connections diminishes and its defensive responses increase. Create a safe context to maximize growth.
- **Facilitate insight.** Learning that originates with the learner is information that sticks. With safe, growth-oriented space and a conversation that is framed as a joint inquiry, rather than a feedback session, the opportunity that new insights will lead to changed thinking, behavior, and attitudes greatly increases.[9]

Making such intentional conversations a regular part of the way work gets done reinforces the core dynamics of the agility shift and builds and expands the ties within your Relational Web.

Recognizing

Every change agent, human resource professional, coach, manager and, let's face it, human being, knows the importance of recognition. I am not talking about the annual awards dinners, quarterly sales bonuses, or other acknowledgements for preset goals, although those can be both motivational and personally satisfying. We can't rely on these methods as a primary means of recognition first and foremost because they relate to planned goals, and secondly because they can inadvertently backfire by demoralizing other worthy employees who did not receive well-deserved public acknowledgement. At the same time, when it comes to the agility shift, it is imperative to recognize effective agile performance: responsiveness to the unplanned, whether it's an opportunity or a challenge. Recognition is also important in the cocreation of a culture of agility, as it amplifies the behaviors, beliefs, and values you want to encourage throughout the organization. Recognition is also important as a means of whole-system feedback, for if we can't recognize agile performance, how will we know if we are doing it? If we don't acknowledge it, how will we continue to be intentional in our agility practices going forward?

There are two more important reasons to recognize agile performance:

1. The brain needs feedback to reinforce learning.
2. People need recognition to sustain engagement, especially in the midst of unpredictable, changing conditions.

Science also supports a shift toward situational recognition. You are likely familiar with the hormone and neurotransmitter dopamine. Its reputation for being released in the midst of pleasurable experiences is long established. Less publicized is dopamine's role in motivation. Neuroscientist Wolfram Schultz and his colleagues at the University of Cambridge have conducted countless studies that show there is actually no evidence of dopamine's release in response to expected rewards, but that dopamine is often released in *anticipation* of a new challenge, to motivate action.[10] While still under study, this evidence supports incremental, unexpected, and positive feedback for agile performance.

The science of the brain also supports Harvard Business School professor and international change expert John Kotter's work spotlighting the need to "celebrate small wins" in any change effort.[11] Without such acknowledgement, teams often begin to lose direction, motivation, and enthusiasm. More recently, his colleague Teresa Amabile and her husband, developmental psychologist Steven Kramer, did in-depth research into significant differentiating factors between high- and low-performing companies by studying the inner work lives of 238 members of creative teams across seven different companies. Confirming Kotter's study, and likely your own experience, Amabile and Kramer found that more than any other factor contributing to sustained team and organizational success was people's experience of positive emotional recognition from making progress on meaningful work.[12] Conversely, those who experienced emotional setbacks at work were two to three times less engaged, committed, and productive. The headline from this in-depth research is that leaders can dramatically enhance engagement and productivity by attuning, attending to, and recognizing the progress their employees and colleagues are making toward meaningful work, while working to remove barriers to such progress. The Make Shift Happen practices below provide specific strategies to support your success.

Make Shift Happen

Ask "How Do You Want to Be Recognized?"

Gather information about meaningful acknowledgements to boost performance and diversify your recognition strategies.

When it comes to recognition, it can be tempting to assume that everyone wants to be recognized the same way. In Western organizations, this often means singling out individuals in public ways, based on the assumption that everyone enjoys his fifteen minutes of fame. This assumption can be problematic for a couple of reasons. Successful agile performance is often based on the effective communication, collaboration, and coordination within the Relational Web, and singling out individual performance can undermine the very dynamics that contribute to agility. Additionally, agile organizations are diverse and increasingly global, made up of people who may be culturally averse to individual and/or public recognition.

There are a number of ways you can be creative and responsive to recognizing agile performance. The onboarding process is a great time to introduce some of the ways you recognize performance in your organization and ask what kinds of recognition have been most meaningful to new hires in their past work experiences. For example, social media shout-outs, weekly meeting shout-outs, newsletter highlights, or a handwritten thank you card from a manager can all resonate differently with employees. It's good to know how new hires feel about these options, since the point of recognizing people is to make them feel good. A best practice is for HR to ask new employees and share feedback with managers, or for managers to ask directly. While it may not be possible to accommodate preferences in every situation, understanding what kind of recognition is meaningful and motivational to each individual can help sustain the level of agile performance you seek.

Catch People in the Act

Shorten the distance between agile performance and recognition to increase engagement and motivation at all levels of the organization.

The shorter the distance between agile performance and recognition, the greater the chance that the recognition will be effective in motivating even more agile performance. Recognition that happens in the midst of, or shortly after, progress and celebrates small wins and accomplishments is often more effective, and less labor intensive, than formal evaluations (not to mention more aligned with the fast pace of agile organizations). Here are a few examples of ways an organization making the agility shift might show recognition:

- Give positive, informal feedback during collaboration.
- Regularly ask the question, "What are we doing well?" in team meetings to recognize positive team dynamics.
- Celebrate the achievement of incremental goals, milestones, and unexpected successes on the way toward larger goals.
- Create a virtual or actual appreciation board that allows anyone to recognize behaviors, attitudes, and random acts of kindness that contribute to the success of the team or organization.

Remember to include support staff in your informal recognition efforts. Though it is sometimes harder to make the direct connection between their good work and business outcomes, you know you could not achieve your goals without them! There is nothing more demoralizing than standing by while the person you made look like a rock star gets inducted into the hall of fame and your role as back-up singer goes unnoticed.

Recognize What You Want to Reinforce

Recognize the skills, knowledge, behaviors, and demeanors that support agile performance to reinforce them at all levels of the organization.

Agile organizations are interested not only in what was accomplished but in *how* it was accomplished. Recognizing both the process and the product of agile performance is essential to reinforcing it and to building a culture in which agility-fostering beliefs, values, and behavior become the norm.

- **Recognize performance indicators.** Use the performance indicators outlined in the table in chapter 8 as a starting point to attune to specific behaviors and outcomes that are aligned with agility.
- **Recognize continuous learning and reflection.** Individual and team learning are essential for sustained agility. Find creative ways to recognize and support this intrinsically motivated behavior by providing additional resources to learning and reflection, such as additional conference and professional development funds.
- **Recognize those who sustain and expand the Relational Web.** One of the best ways to sustain your agility shift is to recognize individuals and teams who creatively engage, sustain, and expand their Relational Web.
- **Recognize new adoptions and adaptations.** For agile organizations, it's not imitation but adoption and adaptation that are the highest forms of flattery. Recognizing newly developed processes and lessons learned in one context that can be more widely adopted or adapted in others is a great way to shine a light on agile performance while reinforcing a culture of organizational learning.

How you recognize what you want to reinforce is not as important as doing so consistently and continuously—and making sure that everyone in the organization shares responsibility for recognizing agile performance.

Retaining

Agile performers stay with agile organizations. Organizations that are making the agility shift are excellent at retaining top talent because they offer an environment where employees can continue learning, developing, and innovating as they take on new challenges.

You also know from your own experience—and the excellent

research of the Gallup organization and Marcus Buckingham and Curt Coffman has confirmed—that people join companies and leave managers.[13] Many agile organizations, however, have moved beyond traditional reporting structures and demand that everyone shares the responsibility for creating a context in which agile performers can thrive. This means that organizations need to be even more intentional in their practices, paying particular attention to the agility shift dynamics, which are the very business and people practices that make agile people want to stay:

- A chance to do work that is relevant to their values and has a clear purpose
- A work environment that is responsive to the changing needs of customers, market, stakeholders, and employees
- An opportunity to work in a context that is resilient, where people quickly regroup and are restored in response to disruptions
- The chance to work with others who are resourceful and to bring out the resourcefulness in one another, to make optimal use of their Relational Web
- A context that is reflective and in which continuous learning is not an afterthought but the way business gets done

And of course, agile people want to belong to and co-create a Relational Web of fellow talented, creative, curious people.

Make Shift Happen

Set People Up for Success

Practice principle number five of "The Agile Manifesto": "Build projects around motivated individuals. Give them the environment and support they need, and trust them to get the job done."[14]

Of course, you must pay attention to this principle as you recruit new employees and assemble your teams by hiring people who have agility competencies, capacity, and confidence, and that is just the start when it comes to retaining agile employees. No one wants to stay in a situation in which he is failing, or cannot work at the top of his talent. Setting people up for success means matching motivated "generalizing specialists" with projects and opportunities that have clear givens and shared agreements about the working process.

It also means providing ample playspace for every member to play with new ideas and try out new roles; for improvised play; and for each player and team to bring their best to the process.[15] This mindset is as key to Ericsson's success in expanding its agile methodologies throughout the organization as it is to small businesses like Mightybytes, which work to match team members with client projects that are relevant to their values and passions. Agility (not to mention innovation and continuous learning) is not achieved through micromanagement. If the promise of your organization is that it is a place where smart, motivated people thrive, you must provide the conditions and resources while trusting them to do the rest. Agile employees stay when the agility promise is kept and they are set up for success by being given room to play.

Coach

Create a coaching culture where everyone shares responsibility for bringing out one another's best performances.

Coaching is not just for the new hire or job changer; it has to be part of the everyday practice. No sports team or individual athlete can expect success by bringing coaches in for only a few early practice sessions, any more than agile leaders, teams, and organizations can expect to sustain their success with occasional guidance. Providing this support does not mean that you need to add yet another line item to your budget or hire a fleet of external coaches. It does mean creating a coaching culture in which all team members understand their role supporting one another's success, as well as the success of each project.

For those using agile methodologies, the scrum master is the one formally charged with keeping the big picture in mind and being sure everyone has the resources and support during each sprint. While the scrum master formally plays the role of coach, she is only as successful as the information she receives during the daily stand-up meetings and sprint reflections. She also needs each member to be in a learning mind-set and be open to her feedback, as well as to the feedback from colleagues. Each of the organizations profiled throughout the book is making the agility shift in large part by creating a coaching culture that demands and embraces continuous learning by all. Agility and innovation depend on it.

Coaching also supports agile success by quickly identifying those who are either unwilling to receive and respond to feedback, or are otherwise not a good fit for the role, project, or organization. If, despite coaching and development, you discover it's the wrong match, cut your losses early. Doing so will reinforce, recognize, and help retain those who are taking responsibility to co-create your success.

The saying goes, "if you do what you've always done, you'll always get what you've always got" (variously attributed to Mark Twain and Henry Ford) and this certainly holds true for recruiting, reinforcing, recognizing, and retaining the agile workforce. If you want to work with people who can think on their feet and easily learn, adapt, and innovate in changing contexts, you need a recruiting and development strategy that is designed to identify and retain this talent. In this chapter, I shared several practices organizations of all sizes and sectors are experimenting with to do just that. I encourage you to adopt this same attitude of experimentation to find the practices that are most successful for your organizational culture and business goals. If you commit to doing things differently, I assure you that you will get different things.

Part Three Summary

It is everyone's job to recruit, reinforce, recognize, and retain agile talent. Agile leaders, teams, and organizations take and share responsibility for their own learning and development. They support others in identifying learning opportunities and generously share their resources and wisdom.

No organization can afford to put the burden for sustaining agile individuals or teams, let alone the entire organization, onto one department or a handful of designated leaders. When everyone shares responsibility for attracting agile talent and supporting their success, you have made the most crucial organizational shift; you have shifted your values, beliefs, and day-to-day behaviors to create a culture in which change and new opportunities are not only welcomed, they are actively pursued.

EPILOGUE

Accepting the Invitation

Each of the leaders, teams, or organizations I have high-lighted in this book accepted the agility shift invitation. They did so because they recognized the business, and human imperative to do so. They each made the shift intentionally, sometimes with a full understanding of the level of commitment required for success, and sometimes with an openness to discover the commitment and resources needed along the way. They *continue* to make this commitment because of the value it is creating and the results they are seeing. Greater levels of employee engagement, communication, collaboration, and coordination are resulting in improved performance. Their leaders and teams are more effective responding to the unexpected and unplanned, and are turning challenges into opportunities more quickly. These organizations also continue to make the agility shift in their mind-set, strategy, and practices not only because they recognize the business value, but because it is a truly exhilarating opportunity.

The agility shift is exhilarating because it calls on each of us to engage at the top of our talent in uncharted waters. When we truly prioritize agility, we also prioritize ways of being in the world that enable agility: ways that create space to move, to play with new ideas, to reflect and respond. We also prioritize being in the dynamic present moment and cultivating the mindfulness necessary for agility.

If you recognize the personal and business value of agility, I invite you to accept this invitation as well. You do not need a master plan, "change management strategy," or the full buy-in from your colleagues or leadership team, to accept. All you need is to recognize the need and opportunity, and to make a commitment to shift your mind-set. With this shift in place, begin to experiment with new ways of working that enhance, rather than impede, your agility and effectiveness within your span of influence. Here, within your thriving web of relationships, you will discover capacities you didn't know you had, create innovative solutions that did not exist, and make a difference beyond your wildest imagination. Soon, you will have others wanting to learn your secrets. *Share them generously.*

APPENDIX A

The Agile Manifesto[1]

1. Our highest priority is to satisfy the customer through early and continuous delivery of valuable software.
2. Welcome changing requirements, even late in development. Agile processes harness change for the customer's competitive advantage.
3. Deliver working software frequently, from a couple of weeks to a couple of months, with a preference to the shorter timescale.
4. Business people and developers must work together daily throughout the project.
5. Build projects around motivated individuals. Give them the environment and support they need, and trust them to get the job done.
6. The most efficient and effective method of conveying information to and within a development team is face-to-face conversation.
7. Working software is the primary measure of progress.
8. Agile processes promote sustainable development. The sponsors, developers, and users should be able to maintain a constant pace indefinitely.
9. Continuous attention to technical excellence and good design enhances agility.

10. Simplicity—the art of maximizing the amount of work not done—is essential.
11. The best architectures, requirements, and designs emerge from self-organizing teams.
12. At regular intervals, the team reflects on how to become more effective, then tunes and adjusts its behavior accordingly.

APPENDIX B

Agility Exercises and Games

Here are a few of my favorite agility exercises and games that can be used in a number of settings, including at the start of a team meeting, during a training session, or as part of the recruiting process. If you have ever taken an improv class you will likely recognize these. To see video demonstrations of these games, as well as additional descriptions visit: pamela-meyer.com

One-Word Story

Invite people to stand, as they are able, and pair up with another person—ideally someone they do not know, or rarely work with. At this point you may choose to lead people through sixty seconds of Be. Here. Now. Time (see next exercise) or simply continue with the game. Instruct players that they are now going to create a story with their partner, a story they haven't heard or told before and that neither of them could have possibly pre-planned. The only rules of the game are that they must alternate from one partner to the other after each word of the story, and that they can only contribute one word at a time. To ensure no one has begun pre-planning, the facilitator can give the pairs their first word, or ask for a suggestion from one of the participants. The first word can be anything "rutabagas," "rainbows," "once," "yesterday," etc. Encourage players to have fun with their story and allow it to go wherever it wants to go. After a round or two in pairs, the facilitator can invite pairs to pair (forming groups of four). For larger groups, you can invite the groups of four to join, and then play a final round with groups of 16 or all participants, standing in a circle, telling a story one word at a time.

This game is helpful to:

- Get participants attuned to each other
- Help everyone experience the dynamic present moment
- Build/assess listening and collaboration skills
- Give people a chance to communicate, collaborate, and coordinate in real time
- Help people make the agility shift and/or assess their agility three Cs (Competence, Capacity, and Confidence)
- Have fun and co-create playspace

Be. Here. Now. Time

This is an excellent exercise to help everyone get in the present moment and back in their bodies. Start by inviting everyone to stand, as they are able. Ask participants to spread out enough to have an arm's length between bodies, if possible. Ask participants to close their eyes, or leave them open with soft focus. Next ask them to take three long extravagant breaths in through their nose, out through their mouth. Invite participants to, refraining from judgment, take a moment to notice what is going on, what they are aware of in their bodies, mental state, emotional state, any other experience they are having. Next invite them to shrug their shoulders up to their earlobes three times, followed by baby shoulder circles that become larger with each rotation (repeat the opposite direction). Then ask everyone to drop their head forward and simply using the weight of their head, gently roll their right ear over their right shoulder and then gently roll the other way with the left ear over the left shoulder (repeat a few times at participants' own pace). Finally, close by inviting everyone to gently bounce up and down, shaking out any last stress, or anything they want to throw away to be fully present. The exercise sounds more complicated than it is.

This game is helpful to:

- Give participants a chance to be in their whole bodies in the dynamic present moment
- Shake off distractions from the day and relax

Transformation Game

This game is a nice alternative to a word game and invites people to use their whole bodies. It can be especially useful in a mixed language group. Participants are asked to form circles of five to six players. One participant is asked to begin the game by using an imaginary object, ideally something they regularly use at home or work. That participant passes the object on to the person to their right who must use the object they are given and then change it into something new. The game continues around the circle with each person accepting the object they are given and transforming it into something new. Participants are instructed in advance that there are two rules: 1) If you don't know what you are being handed, don't accept it and 2) Work in complete silence. After one round, participants are asked to reflect on what they are feeling as the object is being passed around the circle, getting closer and closer to them. Participants are then asked to play another round, this time without planning in advance what they are going to do when the object gets to them, but rather accepting the object they are given and allowing the motion of using that object to transform it into something new. In the second round, the object is passed to the left.

This game is helpful to:

- Build/assess collaboration, communication and coordination skills
- Develop/assess fluency in accepting and building on ideas (Yes, and...)
- Demonstrate and develop the shift from information to interactions
- Create playspace and strengthen the Relational Web

NOTES

Introduction

1. Donald Sull, "Competing Through Organizational Agility," *McKinsey Quarterly* 1 (2010): 48–56.
2. Karl Weick, "The Aesthetic of Imperfection in Orchestras and Organizations," in *Organizational Improvisation,* eds. M. Pina e Cunha, J. Vieira da Cunha, and K.N. Kamoche (New York: Routledge, 2002), 166–84.

Chapter 1

1. Paul D. MacLean, *The Triune Brain in Evolution: Role in Paleocerebral Functions* (New York: Plenum Press, 1990).
2. Bill Faw, "Pre-frontal Executive Committee for Perception, Working Memory, Attention, Long-Term Memory, Motor Control, and Thinking: A Tutorial Review," *Consciousness and Cognition* 12 (2003): 83–139. doi: 10.1016/S1053-8100(02)00030-2.
3. Claudio Ciborra, "Design, Kairos and Affection" (Paper presented at Managing as Designing: Creating a Vocabulary for Management Education and Research, Case-Western Reserve University, Cleveland, OH, June 14–15, 2002).
4. *Apollo 13*, written by Ron Howard (1995; Los Angeles: Universal Pictures, 2006), HD DVD.
5. Marie Glenn "Organisational Agility: How Business Can Survive and Thrive in Turbulent Times" in *Economist Intelligence Unit*, ed. G. Stahl (*Economist*, 2009), 5.
6. Salesforce, *Transforming Your Organization to Agile* (white paper), Salesforce. com (2010), accessed February 14, 2015, https://developer.salesforce.com/page/Transforming_Your_Organization_to_Agile.
7. Kenneth P. De Meuse, Guangrong Dai, and George S. Hallenbeck, "Learning Agility: A Construct Whose Time Has Come," *Consulting Psychology Journal: Practice and Research* 62, no. 2 (2010): 119–30. doi: 10.1037/a0019988.

8. Jeffrey Zaslow, "What We Can Learn from Sully's Journey," Moving On, *Wall Street Journal Online,* last updated October 14, 2009, accessed February 9, 2015, http://www.wsj.com/articles/SB10001424052748703790404574469160016077646.

9. Chesley B. Sullenberger and Jeffrey Zaslow, *Highest Duty: My Search for What Really Matters* (San Francisco: HarperCollins, 2009).

10. Dennis Finn and Anne Donovan, *PwC's NextGen: A Global Generational Study* (PwC, 2013), 1–16.

11. Jeanne Meister and Kari Willyerd, *The 2020 Workplace* (San Francisco: HarperCollins, 2010).

12. Sullenberger, *Highest Duty.*

13. The actual quote attributed to von Moltke is, "Therefore no plan of operations extends with any certainty beyond the first contact with the main hostile force," though it is often truncated (Hughes, 1993, *Moltke on the Art of War: Selected Writings* (Novato, CA: Presidio Press).

14. Steve Denning, "Salesforce CEO Slams the 'The World's Dumbest Idea': Maximizing Shareholder Value," *Forbes,* February 5, 2015, http://www.forbes.com/sites/stevedenning/2015/02/05/salesforce-ceo-slams-the-worlds-dumbest-idea-maximizing-shareholder-value/.

15. David S. Alberts, *The Agility Advantage: A Survival Guide for Complex Enterprises and Endeavors* (Washington D.C.: DoD Command and Control Research Program, 2011).

16. Judith Hicks Stiehm and Nicholas W. Townshend, *The U.S. Army War College: Military Education in a Democracy* (Philadelphia: Temple University Press, 2002).

17. "FAA Releases Transcript from Hudson River Landing," ABC News, February 5, 2009, accessed February 10, 2015, http://abcnews.go.com/Travel/story?id=6802512.

18. Tricia Wachtendorf and James M. Kendra, "Improvising Disaster in the City of Jazz: Organizational Response to Hurricane Katrina," in *Understanding Katrina: Perspectives from the Social Sciences* (June 11, 2006).

Chapter 2

1. Cori Faklaris, "My View of the Washington, Ill., Tornado Disaster," *IndyStar Online,* November 21, 2013, accessed November 29, 2013, http://www.indystar.com/story/news/faklaris/2013/11/21/my-view-of-the-washington-ill-tornado-disaster/3666839/.

2. Stacey Baca and Paul Meincke, "Washington, Illinois Tornado Victims Thankful for Volunteers," ABC7Chicago, accessed November 29, 2013, http://abclocal.go.com/wls/story?section=news/local/illinois&id=9343084.

3. Steven W, Cranford et al., "Nonlinear Material Behaviour of Spider Silk Yields Robust Webs," *Nature* 482 (2012): 72–76, doi: 10.1038/nature10739.

4. Baca, "Washington, Illinois."

5. Dan Buettner, *The Blue Zones: 9 Lessons for Living Longer from the People Who've Lived the Longest*, 2nd ed. (Washington D.C.: National Geographic, 2012).

6. James H. Fowler and Nicholas A. Christakis, "Dynamic Spread of Happiness in a Large Social Network: Longitudinal Analysis Over 20 Years in the Framingham Heart Study," *British Medical Journal* 337(a2338) (2008): 1–9.

7. Louis J. Cozolino, *The Neuroscience of Human Relationships: Attachment and the Developing Social Brain*, 2nd ed. (New York: Norton, 2014), 4.

8. Cozolino, *The Neuroscience of Human Relationships*.

9. Kathleen Taylor, Catherine Marienau and Annalee Lamoreaux. *Using Brain-aware Approaches for Facilitating Adult Learning: Formal and Informal Settings,* (Jossey-Bass, In-press).

10. Steven M. Southwick and Dennis S. Charney, *Resilience: The Science of Mastering Life's Greatest Challenges* (Cambridge UK: Cambridge University Press, 2012).

11. Charles R. Berger and Richard J. Calabrese, "Some Exploration in Initial Interaction and Beyond: Toward a Developmental Theory of Communication," *Human Communication Research* 1 (1975): 99–112.

12. Alexander S. Haslam, et al., "The Collective Origins of Valued Original-ity: A Social Identity Approach to Creativity," *Personality and Social Psychology Review* 17, no. 4 (2013): 384–401, doi: 10.1177/1088868313498001.

13. Michelle Gallardo, "Washington IL Tornado: Football Takes Minds Off Community Devastation; Panther Lose Game, Gain Support, Respect," ABC7Chicago, accessed November 23, 2013, http://abclocal.go.com/wls/story?id=9337711.

Chapter 3

1. Simon Sinek, *Start with Why: How Great Leaders Inspire Everyone to Take Action* (New York: Portfolio, 2011).

2. Freyedon Ahmadi, "Exploring the Casual Relationships Between Organiza-tional Citizenship Behavior, Organizational Agility and Performance," *Inter-disciplinary Journal of Contemporary Research in Business* 3, no. 1 (2011): 618–27.

3. Tim Frick, interview with author, November 15, 2014.

4. Jaqueline M. Stavros and Gina Hinrichs, *SOAR: Building Strength-Based Strat-egy* (Bend, OR: Thin Book Publishing, 2009).

5. David S. Alberts, *The Agility Advantage: A Survival Guide for Complex Enter-prises and Endeavors* (Washington D.C.: DoD Command and Control Research Program, 2011).

6. Alberts, *The Agility Advantage*.

7. Marie Glenn, "Organisational Agility: How Business Can Survive and Thrive in Turbulent Times," in *Economist Intelligence Unit*, ed. G. Stahl (*Economist, 2009*).

8. Raymond Davis and Alan Schrader, *Leading for Growth: How Umpqua Bank Got Cool and Created a Culture of Greatness* (San Francisco: Jossey-Bass, 2007).

9. Joanna N. Mansour, "The Components of a Healthy Culture" (master's thesis, Gonzaga University, Spokana, WA, 2011), 40.

10. Lani Hayward Interview with the author, June 4, 2014.

11. Angela L. Duckworth, Christopher Peterson, Michael D. Matthews, and Dennis R. Kelly, "Grit: Perseverance and Passion for Long-Term Goals," *Journal of Personality and Social Psychology* 92, no. 6 (2007): 1087–101.

12. Steven M. Southwick and Dennis S. Charney, *Resilience: The Science of Mastering Life's Greatest Challenges* (Cambridge, UK: Cambridge University Press, 2012).

13. Karen Reivich and Andrew Shatté, *The Resilience Factor: Seven Keys to Finding Your Inner Strength and Overcoming Life's Hurdles* (New York: Broadway Books, 2003).

14. Almar Latour, "Trial by Fire: A Blaze in Albuquerque Sets Off Major Crisis for Cell-Phone Giants," *Wall Street Journal*, January 29, 2001.

15. Latour, "Trial by Fire."

16. Latour, "Trial by Fire."

17. Andreas Norrman and Ulf Jansson, "Ericsson's Proactive Supply Chain Risk Management Approach After a Serious Sub-Supplier Accident," *International Journal of Physical Distribution & Logistics Management* 34, no. 2 (2004): 450.

18. Norrman, "Ericsson's Proactive Supply Chain Risk Management," 442.

19. Lee Wier, personal communication, December 12, 2013.

20. Laura Stevens and Anna Prior, "UPS Unveils Plans to Improve Delivery Performance," *Wall Street Journal*, January 30, 2014, http://online.wsj.com/news/articles/SB10001424052702303519404579352890602864378.

21. Sarah Halzack, "FedEx, UPS Step Up Their Holiday Shipping Performance," *Washington Post*, January 1, 2015, accessed January 17, 2015, http://www.washingtonpost.com/news/business/wp/2015/01/01/fedex-ups-step-up-their-holiday-shipping-performance/.

22. "The World's Most Valuable Brands List" *Forbes*, April 7, 2015, http://www.forbes.com/powerful-brands/list/

23. Lee Wier, personal communication, December 12, 2013.

24. Karl E. Weick, "The Collapse of Sensemaking: The Mann Gulch Disaster," *Administrative Science Quarterly* 38, no. 4 (1993): 628–52.

25. Weick, "The Collapse of Sensemaking," 636.

26. Matt Ellwell, interview with author, December 18, 2013.

Chapter 4

1. Frank Barrett, *Say Yes to the Mess: Surprising Leadership Lessons from Jazz* (Cambridge, MA:Harvard Business Review, 2012).

2. Ronald S. Burt, "Structural Holes and Good Ideas," *American Journal of Sociology* 110, no. 2 (September 2004): 349–99.

3. Rob Cross and Andrew Parker, *The Hidden Power of Social Networks: Understanding How Work Really Gets Done in Organizations* (Cambridge: Harvard Business School, 2004), 11.

4. Pamela Meyer, "Embodied Learning at Work: Making the Mind-Set Shift from Workplace to Playspace," in *Bodies of Knowledge: Embodied Learning in Adult Education*, ed. R.L. Lawrence (San Francisco: Jossey-Bass, 2012), 25–32.

5. Louis J. Cozolino, *The Neuroscience of Human Relationships: Attachment and the Developing Social Brain*, 2nd ed. (New York: Norton, 2014).

6. Matthew D. Lieberman, *Social: Why Our Brains Are Wired to Connect*, 1st ed. (New York: Crown, 2013).

7. Joseph LeDoux, *Synaptic Self: How Our Brains Become Who We Are* (New York: Viking, 2002).

8. George Lakoff and Mark Johnson, *Metaphors We Live By* (Chicago: University of Chicago Press, 2003).

9. Nils B. Jostmann, Daniël Lakens and Thomas W. Schubert, "Weight as an Embodiment of Importance," *Psychological Science*, 20, no. 9: 1169-1174.

10. Janeen Interlandi, "How Do You Heal a Traumatized Mind," *New York Times Sunday Magazine*, May 25, 2014, 47.

11. Interlandi, "How Do You Heal," 42–58.

12. Howard Gardner, "The Theory of Multiple Intelligences," *Annals of Dyslexia* 37 (1987): 19–35.

13. Harvard Business Review Staff, "Mindfulness in the Age of Complexity," *Harvard Business Review*, accessed January 9, 2015, https://hbr.org/2014/03/mindfulness-in-the-age-of-complexity.

14. "The Mindfulness Business: Western Capitalism Is Looking for Inspiration in Eastern Mysticism," *Economist*, November 16, 2013, 73.

15. Tara Bennett-Goleman, *Emotional Alchemy: How the Mind Can Heal the Heart*, 1st ed. (New York: Harmony Books, 2001), 207–8.

16. Charles R. Berger and Richard J. Calabrese, "Some Exploration in Initial Interaction and Beyond: Toward a Developmental Theory of Communication," *Human Communication Research* 1, no. 2 (1975): 99–112.

17. Jeremy P. Jamieson, Wendy Berry Mendes, and Metthey K. Nock, "Improving Acute Stress Responses: The Power of Reappraisal," *Current Directions in Psychological Science* 22, no. 1 (February 2013): 51–56.

18. Michael M. Lombardo and Robert W. Eichinger, "High Potentials as High Learners," *Human Resource Management* 39, no. 4 (Winter 2000): 321–30.

19. Adam Mitchenson and Robert Morris, Learning About Learning Agility, Greensboro, NC: Center for Creative Leadership, 2012. http:www.ccl.org/Leadership/pdf/research/LearningAgility.pdf

20. Morgan W. McCall, Michael M. Lombardo, and Ann M. Morrison, *Lessons of Experience: How Successful Executives Develop on the Job* (Lexington, MA: Lexington Books, 1988), 34.

21. Corporate Leadership Council, *Realizing the Full Potential of Rising Talent* (Washington, DC: Corporate Executive Board, 2005).

22. Kenneth P. De Meuse, Guangrong Dai, and George S. Hallenbeck, "Learning Agility: A Construct Whose Time Has Come," *Consulting Psychology Journal: Practice and Research* 62, no. 2 (2010): 119–30.

23. Ed O'Boyle and Jim Harter, *The State of the Global Workforce Worldwide* (Washington D.C.: Gallup, Inc., 2013).

Chapter 5

1. Mary Crossan and Rodrick E. White, "The Improvising Organization: Where Planning Meets Opportunity," *Organizing Dynamics* 24, no. 4 (1996): 20.

2. Jeffrey Sweet, *Something Wonderful Right Away: An Oral History of The Second City and The Compass Players*, 2nd ed. (New York: Limelight Books, 1994), 263.

3. Philip H. Mirvis, "Variations on a Theme: Practice Improvisation," *Organization Science* 9, no. 5 (1998): 586–92.

4. Beth A. Bechky and Gerardo Okhuysen, "Expecting the Unexpected? How SWAT Officers and Film Crews Handle Surprises," *Academy of Management Journal* 54, no. 2 (2011): 239–61.

5. Robert C. Ginnett, "Crews as Groups: Their Formation and Their Leadership," in *Cockpit Resource Management*, eds. E.L. Wiener, B.G. Kanki, and R.L. Heimreich (San Diego: Academic, 1993), 71–98.

6. Bechky, "Expecting the Unexpected," 239–61.

7. Bechky, "Expecting the Unexpected," 239–61.

8. Martin Fowler and Jim Highsmith, "The Agile Manifesto," *Software Development Magazine* 9, no. 8 (2001): 29–30.

9. Jeff Sutherland, *Scrum: The Art of Doing Twice the Work in Half the Time* (New York: Crown Business, 2014).

10. James Johnston, "How to Start the Transition from Waterfall to an Agile Process," July 9, 2014, http://www.mightybytes.com/blog/transition-waterfall-to-agile/.

11. Fowler, "The Agile Manifesto," 3.

12. Fowler, "The Agile Manifesto," 3.

13. Yingqin Zheng, Will Venters, and Tony Cornford, "Collective Agility, Paradox and Organizational Improvisation: The Development of a Particle Physics Grids," *Information Systems Journal* 21, no. 4 (2011): 303–33.
14. Philip H. Mirvis, "Variations on a Theme: Practice Improvisation," 588.
15. Fowler, "The Agile Manifesto," 1.
16. Philip H. Mirvis, "Variations on a Theme: Practice Improvisation," 589.
17. Sutherland, *Scrum*, 247.
18. Sutherland, *Scrum*, 15.
19. Sutherland, *Scrum*, 151.
20. LaTodd Williams, phone interview with author, Sept. 15, 2014.
21. Kent Beck et al., "The Agile Manifesto," *Manifesto for Agile Software Development*, 2001, http://www.agilemanifesto.org/.

Chapter 6

1. Lani Hayward, Interview with the author, June 4, 2014.
2. Victor Margolin and Richard Buchanan, eds., *The Idea of Design* (Cambridge, MA: MIT Press, 1995).
3. Rob Cross and Chris Ernst, "Deploying Network Talent to Drive Innovation," *Talent Management* 10, no. 9 (September 2014): 25–27.
4. Maxim Sytch and Adam Tatarynowicz, "Exploring the Locus of Invention: The Dynamics of Network Communities and Firms' Invention Productivity," *Academy of Management Journal* 57, no. 1 (2014): 249–79.
5. Russell J. Funk, "Making the Most of Where You Are: Geography, Networks, and Innovation in Organizations," *Academy of Management Journal* 57, no. 1 (2014): 193–222.
6. Jay R. Galbraith, *Designing Complex Organizations* (Reading, MA: Addison-Wesley, 1972), 2.
7. Harrison Monarth, "A Company Without Job Titles Will Still Have Hierarchies," *Harvard Business Review*, January 28, 2014, http://blogs.hbr.org/2014/01/a-company-without-job-titles-will-still-have-hierarchies/.
8. Christine Moorman and Anne S. Miner, "The Convergence of Planning and Execution: Improvisation in New Product Development," *Journal of Marketing* 62, no. 3 (1998): 1–20.
9. Bill McEvily, Giuseppe Soda, and Marco Tortoriello, "More Formally: Rediscovering the Missing Link Between Formal Organization and Informal Social Structure," *The Academy of Management Annals* 8, no. 1 (2014): 299–345.
10. Georg Schreyögg and Jörg Sydow, "Organizing for Fluidity? Dilemmas of New Organizational Forms," *Organization Science* 21, no. 6 (2010): 1251–62.
11. Ronald S. Burt, "Structural Holes and Good Ideas," *American Journal of Sociology* 110, no. 2 (2004): 349–99.

12. Schreyögg, "Organizing for Fluidity?"

13. Donald Sull, "Competing Through Organizational Agility," *McKinsey Quarterly* 1 (2010): 48–56.

14. LaTodd Williams, personal communication, September 15, 2014.

15. Laura Stevens, "For UPS, E-Commerce Brings Big Business and Big Problems," *Wall Street Journal*, 2014, http://online.wsj.com/articles/for-ups-e-commerce-brings-big-business-and-big-problems-1410489642.

16. Henry Mintzberg and Frances Westley, "Decision Making: It's Not What You Think," *MIT Sloan School of Management Review* 42, no. 3 (2001): 89–93.

17. Mintzberg, "Decision Making," 91.

Chapter 7

1. Marci Jacobs, "Colorado Flood Cost to Top $2 Billion, Eqecat Says," *Bloomberg*, September 9, 2013, accessed November 5, 2014, http://www.bloomberg.com/news/2013-09-20/colorado-flood-cost-to-top-2-billion-eqecat-says.html.

2. Tim Frick, e-mail communication with author, November 5, 2014.

3. James S. Moore, "Predators and Prey: A New Ecology of Competition," *Harvard Business Review* 71, no. 3 (1993): 75–86.

4. James S. Moore, "Business Ecosytems and the View from the Firm," *Antitrust Bulletin* 51, no. 1 (2006): 33.

5. Moore, "Predators and Prey," 79.

6. Moore, "Business Ecosytems," 43.

7. Ram Nidumolu et al., "The Collaboration Imperative," *Harvard Business Review* 94, no. 2 (2014): 76–84.

8. Rosabeth Moss Kanter, "Enrich the Ecosystem: A Four-Point Plan for Linking Innovation, Enterprises, and Jobs," *Harvard Business Review* (March 2012): 141–47.

9. Chris Nyren, "About Us," Educelerate, accessed October 20, 2014, https://angel.co/educelerate.

10. "History," SCU Center for Science, Technology, and Society, accessed October 20, 2014, http://www.scu.edu/socialbenefit/about/history/.

11. Adam Lugwig, "Don't Call It Crowd-Sourcing: Quirky CEO Ben Kaufman Brings Invention to the Masses," *Forbes*, April 23, 2012, accessed February 16, 2015, http://www.forbes.com/sites/techonomy/2012/04/23/dont-call-it-crowdsourcing-quirky-ceo-ben-kaufman-brings-invention-to-the-masses/.

12. Pamela Meyer, *From Workplace to Playspace: Innovating, Learning and Changing Through Dynamic Engagement* (San Francisco: Jossey-Bass, 2010).

13. Vijith Assar, "Software that Builds Software," *New Yorker*, August 7, 2013, accessed February 16, 2015, http://www.newyorker.com/tech/elements/the-software-that-builds-software.

14. John Markoff, "In a Video Game, Tackling the Complexities of Protein Folding," *New York Times,* August 5, 2010, accessed February 16, 2015, http://www.nytimes.com/2010/08/05/science/05protein.html?_r=0.

15. "Umpqua Bank Connect Volunteer Network Marks 10 Years of Community Engagement," January 30, 2015. https://www.umpquabank.com/news-and-murmurs/10-years-community-engagement-013014/

16. Alyson Warhurst, "Humanitarian Teamwork from Logistics Giants," *BusinessWeek Online,* January 25, 2008, http://www.bloomberg.com/bw/stories/2008-01-25/humanitarian-teamwork-from-logistics-giantsbusinessweek-business-news-stock-market-and-financial-advice.

17. Ericsson, "New Millennium Village in Ghana to be Supported by Ericsson and Tigo Technology," *Millennium Villages,* May 21, 2012, accessed January 23, 2015, http://millenniumvillages.org/press-releases/new-millennium-village-in-ghana-to-be-supported-by-ericsson-and-tigo-technology/.

18. James S. Moore, *The Death of Competition: Leadership and Strategy in the Age of Business Ecosystems* (San Francisco: HarperBusiness, 1996).

19. Maxim Sytch and Adam Tatarynowicz, "Exploring the Locus of Invention: The Dynamics of Network Communities and Firms' Invention Productivity," *Academy of Management Journal* 57, no. 1 (2014): 249–79.

20. Rosabeth M. Kanter, "Enrich the Ecosystem," 141–47.

Chapter 8

1. Anne Schwartz, interview with author, August 8, 2014.

2. Anne Schwartz, interview with author.

3. Peter Park, "Knowledge and Participatory Research," in *Handbook of Action Research,* eds. P. Reason and H. Bradbury (London: Sage, 2001), 81–90.

4. Paulo Freire, *Pedagogy of the Oppressed* (New York: Continuum, 1979).

5. David S. Alberts, *The Agility Advantage: A Survival Guide for Complex Enterprises and Endeavors* (Washington D.C.: DoD Command and Control Research Program, 2011).

6. Kwang Kim, Mary Hagedorn, Jennifer Williamson, and Christopher Chapman, *Participation in Adult Education and Lifelong Learning: 2000–01* (Washington D.C.: U.S. Department of Education, National Center for Education Statistics, 2004).

7. Enoch A. Awoniyi, Orlando V. Griego, and George A. Morgan, "Person-Environment Fit and Transfer of Training," *International Journal of Training and Development* 6 (2002): 25–35;

8. David A. Kolb, *Experiential Learning: Experience as the Source of Learning and Development* (Englewood Cliffs, NJ: Prentice Hall, 1984);

9. Kenneth P. De Meuse, *What's Smarter than IQ? Learning Agility* (Los Angeles: Korn Ferry Institute, 2013);

10. Kenneth P. De Meuse, Guangrong Dai, and George S. Hallenbeck, "Learning Agility: A Construct Whose Time Has Come," *Consulting Psychology Journal: Practice and Research* 62, no. 2 (2010): 121, doi: 10.1037/a0019988.

11. Carl Straumsheim, "Flipping Med Ed," *Inside Higher Ed*, September 9, 2013, https://www.insidehighered.com/news/2013/09/09/stanford-university-and -khan-academy-use-flipped-classroom-medical-education.

12. Scott W. Ambler, "Generalizing Specialists: Improving Your IT Career Skills," *Agile Modeling*, accessed November 19, 2014, http://agilemodeling .com/essays/generalizingSpecialists.htm.

13. McCall, *Lessons of Experience*.

14. Michael W. Allen and Richard Sites, *Leaving ADDIE for SAM: An Agile Model for Developing the Best Learning Experiences* (Alexandria, VA: ASTD, 2012).

15. Saranne Magennis and Alison Farrell, "Teaching and Learning Activities: Expanding the Repertoire to Support Student Learning," in *Emerging Issues in the Practice of University Learning and Teaching*, eds. G. O'Neill, S. Moore, and B. McMullin (Dublin: All Ireland Society for Higher Education/Higher Education Authority, 2005).

16. Allen, *Leaving ADDIE for SAM*.

17. Pamela Meyer, *Quantum Creativity: Nine Principles to Transform the Way You Work* (Chicago: Contemporary Books, 2000);

18. Jeff Sutherland, *Scrum: The Art of Doing Twice the Work in Half the Time* (New York: Crown Business, 2014).

19. Nick Carey, "Gasoline Price Drop Could Boost U.S. Holiday Spending: UPS CFO," *Reuters*, November 11, 2014, accessed December 8, 2014, http://www.reuters.com/article/2014/11/18/us-ups-cfo-gas-consumers -idUSKCN0J221T20141118.

20. Philip H. Mirvis, "Variations on a Theme: Practice Improvisation," *Organization Science* 9 (1998): 578.

21. Martin P. Paulusa et al., "A Neuroscience Approach to Optimizing Brain Resources for Human Performance in Extreme Environments," *Neuroscience & Biobehavioral Review* 33, no. 7 (2009): 1080–88.

22. Richard T. Watson et al., "Telematics at UPS: En Route to Energy Informatics," *MIS Quarterly* 9, no. 1 (2010): 1–11.

23. John Dix, "How UPS Uses Analytics to Drive Down Costs (and No, It Doesn't Call It Big Data), *CIO.com*, December 1, 2014, accessed December 6, 2014, http://www.cio.com/article/2852509/data-analytics/how-ups-uses-analytics -to-drive-down-costs-and-no-it-doesnt-call-it-big-data.html.

24. Etienne Wenger, Richard McDermott, and William Snyder, *Cultivating Communities of Practice* (Cambridge, MA: Harvard Business School Press, 2002).

25. Wenger, *Cultivating Communities*.

Chapter 9

1. Sharon Florentine, "How To Attract Agile Development Talent," *CIO.com*, September 15, 2014, accessed December 11, 2014, http://www.cio.com/article /2683242/careers-staffing/how-to-attract-agile-development-talent.html.

2. Philip Mirvis, "Variations on a Theme: Practice Improvisation," *Organization Science* 9 (1998): 586–92.

3. Gregory Ferenstein, "Eric Schmidt on the Special Trait of Google's Top Talent and How to Attract Them (in 3 Quotes)," *VB News*, October 14, 2014, accessed December 12, 2014, http://venturebeat.com/2014/10/14/eric -schmidt-on-the-special-trait-of-googles-top-talent-and-how-to-attract -them-in-3-quotes/.

4. Rita Pyrllis, "How Mobile Delivers Talent for Ups," *Talent Management* 10 (2014): 45–49.

5. Carol Semrad, interview with author, October 20, 2014.

6. Sarah Sipek, "A Return to Qualitative," *Talent Management* 10 (2014): 16–19.

7. Susan Ladika, "Collaborative Edge," *HR* magazine 59 (2014): 37–40, 42.

8. David Rock, "SCARF: A Brain-Based Model for Collaborating With and Influencing Others," *Neuroleadership Journal* 1, no. 1 (2008): 78–87.

9. David Rock, "Transforming the Quality of Development Conversations at Scale," *Chief Learning Officer Webinars*, Webinar, December 31, 2014, http:// www.slideshare.net/humancapitalmedia/transforming-the-quality-of -development-conversations-at-scale-42647913.

10. Jeffrey R. Hollerman and Wolfram Schultz, "Dopamine Neurons Report an Error in the Temporal Prediction of Reward During Learning," *Nat Neurosci* 1, no. 4 (1998): 304–9.

11. John Kotter, "Leading Change: Why Transformation Efforts Fail," *Harvard Business Review Best of HBR 2006* (2006): 1–10.

12. Teresa M. Amabile and Steven J. Kramer, *The Progress Principle: Using Small Wins to Ignite Joy, Engagement and Creativity at Work* (Cambridge, MA: Harvard Business Review, 2011).

13. Marcus Buckingham and Curt Coffman, *First Break All the Rules* (New York: Simon & Schuster, 1999).

14. Martin Fowler and Jim Highsmith, "The Agile Manifesto," *Software Development* 9 (2001): 29–30.

15. Pamela Meyer, *From Workplace to Playspace: Innovating, Learning and Changing Through Dynamic Engagement* (San Francisco: Jossey-Bass, 2010).

Appendix A

1. Kent Beck, et al. (2001). "The Principles Behind the Agile Manifesto." Retrieved July 10, 2015, from http://agilemanifesto.org/principles.html.

REFERENCES

Ahmadi, Freyedon. "Exploring the Casual Relationships Between Organizational Citizenship Behavior, Organizational Agility and Performance." *Interdisciplinary Journal of Contemporary Research in Business* 3, no. 1 (2011).

Alberts, David S. *The Agility Advantage: A Survival Guide for Complex Enterprises and Endeavors.* Washington D.C.: DoD Command and Control Research Program, 2011.

Allen, Michael W., and Richard Sites. *Leaving ADDIE for SAM: An Agile Model for Developing the Best Learning Experiences.* Alexandria, VA: ASTD, 2012.

Amabile, Teresa M., and Steven J. Kramer. *The Progress Principle: Using Small Wins to Ignite Joy, Engagement and Creativity at Work.* Cambridge, MA: Harvard Business Review, 2011.

Ambler, Scott W. "Generalizing Specialists: Improving Your IT Career Skills." *Agile Modeling.* Accessed November 19, 2014. http://agilemodeling.com/essays/generalizingSpecialists.htm.

Apollo 13. Written by Ron Howard. 1995. Los Angeles: Universal Pictures, 2006. HD DVD.

Assar, Vijith. "Software that Builds Software." *The New Yorker,* August 7, 2013. Accessed February 16, 2015. http://www.newyorker.com/tech/elements/the-software-that-builds-software.

Awoniyi, E.A., O.V. Griego, and G.A. Morgan. "Person-Environment Fit and Transfer of Training." *International Journal of Training and Development* 6 (2002).

Baca, Stacey, and Paul Meincke. "Washington, Illinois Tornado Victims Thankful for Volunteers." ABC/Chicago, November 28, 2013. Accessed November 29, 2013. http://abclocal.go.com/wls/story?section=news/local/illinois&id=9343084

Barrett, Frank. *Yes to the Mess: Surprising Leadership Lessons from Jazz.* Cambridge, MA: Harvard Business Review, 2012.

Bechky, Beth A., and Gerardo Okhuysen. "Expecting the Unexpected? How SWAT Officers and Film Crews Handle Surprises." *Academy of Management Journal* 54, no. 2 (2011).

Beck, Kent, Mike Beedle, Arie van Bennekum, Alistair Cockburn, Ward Cunningham, Martin Fowler, James Grenning, Jim Highsmith, Andrew Hunt, Ron Jeffries, Jon Kern, Brian Marick, Robert C. Martin, Steve Mellor, Ken Schwaber, Jeff Sutherland, and Dave Thomas. "The Agile Manifesto." *Manifesto for Agile Software Development*, 2001. http://www.agilemanifesto.org/.

Bennett-Goleman, Tara. *Emotional Alchemy: How the Mind Can Heal the Heart*, 1st ed. New York: Harmony Books, 2001.

Berger, Charles R., and Richard J. Calabrese. "Some Exploration in Initial Interaction and Beyond: Toward a Developmental Theory of Communication." *Human Communication Research* 1, no. 2 (1975).

Buckingham, Marcus and Curt Coffman. *First Break All the Rules*. New York: Simon & Schuster, 1999.

Buettner, Dan. *The Blue Zones: 9 Lessons for Living Longer from the People Who've Lived the Longest,* 2nd ed. Washington D.C.: National Geographic, 2012.

Burt, Ronald S. "Structural Holes and Good Ideas." *American Journal of Sociology* 110, no. 2 (2004).

Carey, Nick "Gasoline Price Drop Could Boost U.S. Holiday Spending: UPS CFO." Reuters. Accessed December 8, 2014. http://www.reuters.com/article/2014/11/18/us-ups-cfo-gas-consumers-idUSKCN0J221T20141118.

Ciborra, Claudio. "Design, Kairos and Affection." Presented at Managing as Designing: Creating a Vocabulary for Management Education and Research, Case-Western Reserve University, Cleveland, OH, June 14–15, 2002.

Cox, Milton D. "Fostering the Scholarship and Teaching Through Faculty Learning Communities." *Excellence in College Teaching* 14, no. (February 3, 2003).

Cozolino, Louis J. *The Neuroscience of Human Relationships: Attachment and the Developing Social Brain*, 2nd ed. New York: Norton, 2014.

Cranford, Steven W., Anna Tarakanova, Nicola M. Pugno, and Markus J. Buehler. "Nonlinear Material Behaviour of Spider Silk Yields Robust Webs." *Nature* 482 (2012). doi: 10.1038/nature10739.

Cross, Rob, and Andrew Parker. *The Hidden Power of Social Networks: Understanding How Work Really Gets Done in Organizations*. Cambridge: Harvard Business School, 2004.

Cross, Rob, and Chris Ernst. "Deploying Network Talent to Drive Innovation." *Talent Management* 10, no. 9 (September 2014).

Crossan, Mary, and Rodrick E. White. "The Improvising Organization: Where Planning Meets Opportunity." *Organizing Dynamics* 24, no. 4 (1996).

Davis, Raymond, and Alan Schrader. *Leading for Growth: How Umpqua Bank Got Cool and Created a Culture of Greatness*. San Francisco: Jossey-Bass, 2007.

De Meuse, Kenneth P. *What's Smarter than IQ? Learning Agility*. Los Angeles: Korn Ferry Institute, 2013.

De Meuse, Kenneth P., Guangrong Dai, and George S. Hallenbeck. "Learning

Agility: A Construct Whose Time Has Come." *Consulting Psychology Journal: Practice and Research* 62, no. 2 (2010). doi: 10.1037/a0019988.

Denning, Steve. "Salesforce CEO Slams the 'The World's Dumbest Idea': Maximizing Shareholder Value." *Forbes,* February 5, 2015. http://www.forbes.com/sites/stevedenning/2015/02/05/salesforce-ceo-slams-the-worlds-dumbest-idea-maximizing-shareholder-value/.

Dix, John. "How UPS Uses Analytics to Drive Down Costs (and No, It Doesn't Call It Big Data)." *CIO Online,* December 1, 2014. Accessed December 6, 2014. http://www.cio.com/article/2852509/data-analytics/how-ups-uses-analytics-to-drive-down-costs-and-no-it-doesnt-call-it-big-data.html.

Duckworth, Angela L., Christopher Peterson, Michael D. Matthews, and Dennis R. Kelly. "Grit: Perseverance and Passion for Long-Term Goals." *Journal of Personality and Social Psychology* 92, no. 6 (2007).

Ellwell, Matt. Interview with author, December 18, 2013.

"FAA Releases Transcript from Hudson River Landing." *ABC News,* February 5, 2009. Accessed February 10, 2015. http://abcnews.go.com/Travel/story?id=6802512.

Faklaris, Cori. "My View of the Washington, Ill., Tornado Disaster." *IndyStar Online,* November 22, 2013. Accessed November 29, 2013. http://www.indystar.com/story/news/faklaris/2013/11/21/my-view-of-the-washington-ill-tornado-disaster/3666839/.

Faw, Bill. "Pre-frontal Executive Committee for Perception, Working Memory, Attention, Long-Term Memory, Motor Control, and Thinking: A Tutorial Review." *Consciousness and Cognition* 12 (2003). doi: 10.1016/S1053-8100(02)00030-2.

Ferenstein, Gregory. "Eric Schmidt on the Special Trait of Google's Top Talent and How to Attract Them (in 3 Quotes)." *VB News,* October 14, 2014. Accessed December 12, 2014. http://venturebeat.com/2014/10/14/eric-schmidt-on-the-special-trait-of-googles-top-talent-and-how-to-attract-them-in-3-quotes/.

Finn, Dennis, and Anne Donovan. *PwC's NextGen: A Global Generational Study.* PwC, 2013.

Florentine, Sharon. "How to Attract Agile Development Talent." *CIO Online,* September 15, 2014. Accessed December 11, 2014. http://www.cio.com/article/2683242/careers-staffing/how-to-attract-agile-development-talent.html.

Fowler, James H., and Nicholas A. Christakis. "Dynamic Spread of Happiness in a Large Social Network: Longitudinal Analysis Over 20 Years in the Framingham Heart Study." *British Medical Journal* 337(a2338) (2008).

Fowler, Martin, and Jim Highsmith. "The Agile Manifesto." *Software Development* magazine 9, no. 8 (2001).

Freire, Paulo. *Pedagogy of the Oppressed.* New York: Continuum, 1979.

Frick, Tim. E-mail communication with author, November 5, 2014.

Frick, Tim. Interview with author, November 15, 2014.

Funk, Russell J. "Making the Most of Where You Are: Geography, Networks, and Innovation in Organizations." *Academy of Management Journal* 57, no. 1 (2014).

Galbraith, Jay R. *Designing Complex Organizations*. Reading, MA: Addison-Wesley, 1972.

Gallardo, Michelle. "Washington IL Tornado: Football Takes Minds Off Community Devastation; Panther Lose Game, Gain Support, Respect." ABC-7Chicago, November 23, 2013. Accessed November 23, 2013. http://abclocal.go.com/wls/story?id=9337711.

Gardner, Howard. "The Theory of Multiple Intelligences." *Annals of Dyslexia* 37 (1987).

Ginnett, Robert C. "Crews as Groups: Their Formation and Their Leadership." In *Cockpit Resource Management*, edited by. E.L. Wiener, B.G. Kanki, and R.L. Heimreich. San Diego: Academic, 1993.

Glenn, Marie. "Organisational Agility: How Business Can Survive and Thrive in Turbulent Times." In *Economist Intelligence Unit*, edited by G. Stahl. *Economist*, 2009.

Halzack, Sarah. "FedEx, UPS Step Up Their Holiday Shipping Performance." *Washington Post*, January 1, 2015. Accessed January 17, 2015. http://www.washingtonpost.com/news/business/wp/2015/01/01/fedex-ups-step-up-their-holiday-shipping-performance/.

Harvard Business Review Staff. "Mindfulness in the Age of Complexity." *Harvard Business Review*, March 2014. Accessed January 9, 2015. https://hbr.org/2014/03/mindfulness-in-the-age-of-complexity.

Haslam, S. Alexander, Inmaculada Adarves-Yorno, Tom Postmes, and Lise Jans. "The Collective Origins of Valued Originality: A Social Identity Approach to Creativity." *Personality and Social Psychology Review* 17, no. 4 (2013). doi: 10.1177/1088868313498001.

Hayward, Lani, EVP/Creative Strategies at Umpqua Bank. Interview with the author, June 4, 2014.

"History." *SCU Center for Science, Technology, and Society*. Accessed October 20, 2014. http://www.scu.edu/socialbenefit/about/history/.

Hollerman, Jeffrey R., and Wolfram Schultz. "Dopamine Neurons Report an Error in the Temporal Prediction of Reward During Learning." *Nat Neurosci* 1, no. 4 (1998).

Interlandi, Jeneen. "How Do You Heal a Traumatized Mind?" *New York Times Magazine*. May 22, 2014.

Jacobs, Marci. "Colorado Flood Cost to Top $2 Billion, Eqecat Says." Bloomberg, September 20, 2013. Accessed November 5, 2014. http://www.bloomberg.com/news/2013-09-20/colorado-flood-cost-to-top-2-billion-eqecat-says.html.

Jamieson, Jeremy P., Wendy Berry Mendes, and Metthey K. Nock. "Improving

Acute Stress Responses: The Power of Reappraisal." *Current Directions in Psychological Science* 22, no. 1 (February 2013).

Johnston, James. "How to Start the Transition from Waterfall to an Agile Process." *Mightybytes Blog,* July 9, 2014. http://www.mightybytes.com/blog/transition-waterfall-to-agile/.

Jostman, Nils B., Daniël Lakens, Thomas W. Shubert. "Weight as an Embodiment of Importance." *Psychological Science* 20, no. 9 (September 2009).

Kim, Kwang, Mary Hagedorn, Jennifer Williamson, and Christopher Chapman. *Participation in Adult Education and Lifelong Learning: 2000–01.* Washington D.C.: U.S. Department of Education, National Center for Education Statistics, 2004.

Kolb, David A. *Experiential Learning: Experience as the Source of Learning and Development.* Englewood Cliffs, NJ: Prentice Hall, 1984.

Kotter, John. "Leading Change: Why Transformation Efforts Fail." *Harvard Business Review Best of HBR 2006.*

Ladika, Susan. "Collaborative Edge." *HR* magazine 59 (2014).

Lakoff, George, and Mark Johnson. *Metaphors We Live By.* Chicago: University of Chicago Press, 2003.

Latour, Almar. "Trial by Fire: A Blaze in Albuquerque Sets Off Major Crisis for Cell-Phone Giants." *Wall Street Journal,* January 29, 2001.

LeDoux, Joseph. *Synaptic Self: How Our Brains Become Who We Are.* New York: Viking, 2002.

Lieberman, Matthew D. *Social: Why Our Brains Are Wired to Connect,* 1st ed. New York: Crown, 2013.

Lombardo, Michael M., and Robert W. Eichinger. "High Potentials as High Learners." *Human Resource Management* 39 (2000).

Lugwig, Adam. "Don't Call It Crowd-Sourcing: Quirky CEO Ben Kaufman Brings Invention to the Masses." *Forbes,* April 23, 2014. Accessed February 16, 2015. http://www.forbes.com/sites/techonomy/2012/04/23/dont-call-it-crowdsourcing-quirky-ceo-ben-kaufman-brings-invention-to-the-masses/.

MacLean, Paul D. *The Triune Brain in Evolution: Role in Paleocerebral Functions.* New York: Plenum Press, 1990.

Magennis, Saranne, and Alison Farrell. "Teaching and Learning Activities: Expanding the Repertoire to Support Student Learning." In *Emerging Issues in the Practice of University Learning and Teaching,* edited by G. O'Neill, S. Moore, and B. McMullin. Dublin: All Ireland Society for Higher Education/Higher Education Authority, 2005.

Mansour, Joanna N. "The Components of a Healthy Culture." Master's thesis. Gonzaga University, Spokana, WA, 2011.

Margolin, Victor, and Richard Buchanan, eds. *The Idea of Design.* Cambridge, MA: MIT Press, 1995.

Markoff, John. "In a Video Game, Tackling the Complexities of Protein Folding." *New York Times,* August 5, 2010. Accessed February 16, 2015. http://www.nytimes.com/2010/08/05/science/05protein.html?_r=0.

McCall, Morgan W., Michael M. Lombardo, and Ann M. Morrison. *Lessons of Experience: How Successful Executives Develop on the Job.* Lexington, MA: Lexington Books, 1988.

McEvily, Bill, Guiseppe Soda, and Marco Tortoriello. "More Formally: Rediscovering the Missing Link Between Formal Organization and Informal Social Structure." *The Academy of Management Annals* 8, no. 1 (2014).

Meister, Jeanne, and Kari Willyerd. *The 2020 Workplace.* San Francisco: HarperCollins, 2010.

Meyer, Pamela "Embodied Learning at Work: Making the Mind-Set Shift from Workplace to Playspace. In *Bodies of Knowledge: Embodied Learning in Adult Education,* edited by R.L. Lawrence. San Francisco: Jossey-Bass, 2012.

Meyer, Pamela. *From Workplace to Playspace: Innovating, Learning and Changing Through Dynamic Engagement.* San Francisco: Jossey-Bass, 2010.

Meyer, Pamela. *Quantum Creativity: Nine Principles to Transform the Way You Work.* Chicago: Contemporary Books, 2000.

Mintzberg, Henry, and Frances Westley. "Decision Making: It's Not What You Think." *MIT Sloan School of Management Review* 42, no. 3 (2001).

Mirvis, Philip H. "Variations on a Theme: Practice Improvisation." *Organization Science* 9, no. 5 (1998).

Mitchinson, Adam, and Robert Morris. *Learning About Learning Agility.* Greensboro, NC: Center for Creative Leadership, 2012. http://www.ccl.org/Leadership/pdf/research/LearningAgility.pdf.

Monarth, Harrison. "A Company Without Job Titles Will Still Have Hierarchies." *Harvard Business Review,* 2014. http://blogs.hbr.org/2014/01/a-company-without-job-titles-will-still-have-hierarchies/.

Moore, James S. "Business Ecosytems and the View from the Firm." *Antitrust Bulletin* 51, no. 1 (2006).

Moore, James S. "Predators and Prey: A New Ecology of Competition." *Harvard Business Review* 71, no. 3 (1993).

Moore, James S. *The Death of Competition: Leadership and Strategy in the Age of Business Ecosystems.* San Francisco: HarperBusiness, 1996.

Moorman, Christine, and Anne S. Miner. "The Convergence of Planning and Execution: Improvisation in New Product Development." *Journal of Marketing* 62, no. 3 (1998).

Moss Kanter, Rosabeth. "Enrich the Ecosystm: A Four-Point Plan for Linking Innovation, Enterprises and Jobs." *Harvard Business Review* (March 2012).

Nidumolu, Ram, Jib Ellison, John Whalen, and Erin Billman. "The Collaboration Imperative." *Harvard Business Review* 94, no. 2 (2014).

Norrman, Andreas, and Ulf Jansson. "Ericsson's Proactive Supply Chain Risk Management Approach After a Serious Sub-Supplier Accident." *International Journal of Physical Distribution & Logistics Management* 34, no. 2 (2004).

Nyren, Chris. "About Us." Educelerate. Accessed October 20, 2014, https://angel.co/educelerate.

O'Boyle, Ed, and Jim Harter. *The State of the Global Workforce Worldwide.* Washington D.C.: Gallup, Inc., 2013.

Park, Peter. "Knowledge and Participatory Research." In *Handbook of Action Research*, edited by P. Reason and H. Bradbury. London: Sage, 2001.

Paulusa, Martin P., Eric G. Potterat, Marcus K. Taylor, Karl F. Van Orden, James Bauman, Nausheen Momen, Genieleah A. Padilla, and Judith L. Swain. "A Neuroscience Approach to Optimizing Brain Resources for Human Performance in Extreme Environments." *Neuroscience & Biobehavioral Review* 33, no. 7 (2009).

Pyrllis, Rita. "How Mobile Delivers Talent for UPS." *Talent Management* 10 (2014).

"Realizing the Full Potential of Rising Talent." *Corporate Executive Board Report.* Corporate Leadership Council, 2005.

Reivich, Karen, and Andrew Shatté. *The Resilience Factor: Seven Keys to Finding Your Inner Strength and Overcoming Life's Hurdles.* New York: Broadway Books, 2003.

Rock, David. "SCARF: A Brain-Based Model for Collaborating with and Influencing Others." *Neuroleadership Journal* 1, no. 1 (2008).

Rock, David. "Transforming the Quality of Development Conversations at Scale." *Chief Learning Officer Webinars.* Webinar. December 31, 2014. http://www.slideshare.net/humancapitalmedia/transforming-the-quality-of-development-conversations-at-scale-42647913.

Saks, Alan M., and Monica Belcourt. "An Investigation of Training Activities and Transfer of Training in Organizations." *Human Resource Management* 45, no. 4 (2006).

Salesforce. "Transforming your Organization to Agile." (White paper). Salesforce.com, 2010. Accessed February 14, 2015. https://developer.salesforce.com/page/Transforming_Your_Organization_to_Agile.

Schreyögg, Georg, and Jörg Sydow. "Organizing for Fluidity? Dilemmas of New Organizational Forms." *Organization Science* 21, no. 6 (2010).

Schwartz, A. Personal communication. August 8, 2014.

Semrad, Carol. Interview with author. October 20, 2014.

Sinek, Simon. *Start with Why: How Great Leaders Inspire Everyone to Take Action.* New York: Portfolio, 2011.

Sipek, Sarah. "A Return to Qualitative." *Talent Management* 10 (2014).

Southwick, Steven M., and Dennis S. Charney. *Resilience: The Science of Mastering Life's Greatest Challenges.* Cambridge UK: Cambridge University Press, 2012.

Stavros, Jaqueline M., and Gina Hinrichs. *SOAR: Building Strength-Based Strategy*. Bend, OR: Thin Book Publishing, 2009.

Stevens, Laura, and Anna Prior. "UPS Unveils Plans to Improve Delivery Performance." *Wall Street Journal*, January 30, 2014. http://online.wsj.com/news/articles/SB10001424052702303519404579352890602864378.

Stevens, Laura. "For UPS, E-Commerce Brings Big Business and Big Problems." *Wall Street Journal*, September 11, 2014. http://online.wsj.com/articles/for-ups-e-commerce-brings-big-business-and-big-problems-1410489642.

Stiehm, Judith Hicks, and Nicholas W. Townshend. *The U.S. Army War College: Military Education in a Democracy*. Philadelphia: Temple University Press, 2002.

Straumsheim, Carl. "Flipping Med Ed." *Inside Higher Ed*, September 9, 2013. https://www.insidehighered.com/news/2013/09/09/stanford-university-and-khan-academy-use-flipped-classroom-medical-education.

Sull, Donald. "Competing Through Organizational Agility." *McKinsey Quarterly* 1 (2010).

Sullenberger, Chesley B., and Jeffrey Zaslow. *Highest Duty: My Search for What Really Matters*. San Francisco: HarperCollins, 2009.

Sutherland, Jeff. *Scrum: The Art of Doing Twice the Work in Half the Time*. New York: Crown Business, 2014.

Sweet, Jeffrey. *Something Wonderful Right Away: An Oral History of The Second City and The Compass Players*, 2nd ed. New York: Limelight Books, 1994.

Sytch, Maxim, and Adam Tatarynowicz. "Exploring the Locus of Invention: The Dynamics of Network Communities and Firms' Invention Productivity." *Academy of Management Journal* 57, no. 1 (2014).

Taylor, Kathleen, Catherine Marienau and Annalee Lamoreaux. *Using Brain-aware Approaches for Facilitating Adult Learning: Formal and Informal Settings, In-press, San Francisco: Jossey-Bass, 2016.*

"The Mindfulness Business: Western Capitalism Is Looking for Inspiration in Eastern Mysticism." *Economist*, November 16, 2013.

"Umpqau Bank Connect Volunteer Network Marks 10 Years of Community Engagement," Retrieved May 20, 2015. https://www.umpquabank.com/news-and-murmurs/10-years-community-engagement-013014/

"UPS Rises on List of 2014 Most Valuable Global Brands." *Wall Street Journal*, April 7, 2014. http://online.wsj.com/article/PR-CO-20140224-910503.html.

Von Moltke, Helmuth. *Moltke on the Art of War: Selected Writings*, edited by Daniel Hughes. Novato, CA: Presidio Press, 1993.

Wachtendorf, Tricia, and James M. Kendra. "Improvising Disaster in the City of Jazz: Organizational Response to Hurricane Katrina." *Understanding Katrina: Perspectives from the Social Sciences* (June 11, 2006).

Warhurst, Alyson. "Humanitarian Teamwork from Logistics Giants." *Business-Week Online,* January 25, 2008. http://www.bloomberg.com/bw/stories/

2008-01-25/humanitarian-teamwork-from-logistics-giantsbusinessweek
-business-news-stock-market-and-financial-advice.

Watson, Richard T., Marie-Claude Boudreau, Seth Li, and Jack Levis Jack. "Telematics at UPS: En Route to Energy Informatics." *MIS Quarterly* 9, no. 1 (2010).

Weick, Karl E. "The Collapse of Sensemaking: The Mann Gulch Disaster." *Administrative Science Quarterly* 38, no. 4 (1993).

Weick, Karl E. "The Aesthetic of Imperfection in Orchestras and Organizations." In *Organizational Improvisation*, edited by M. Pina e Cunha, J. Vieira da Cunha, and K.N. Kamoche. New York: Routledge, 2002.

Wenger, Etienne, Richard McDermott, and William Snyder. *Cultivating Communities of Practice*. Cambridge, MA: Harvard Business School Press, 2002.

Wier, Lee Personal communication. December 12, 2013.

Williams, LaTodd. Interview with the author. September 15, 2014.

Zaslow, Jeffrey. "What We Can Learn from Sully's Journey." *Moving On, Wall Street Journal Online,* October 14, 2009. Accessed February 9, 2015. http://www.wsj.com/articles/SB10001424052748703790404574469160016077646.

Zheng, Yingqin, Will Venters, and Tony Cornford. "Collective Agility, Paradox and Organizational Improvisation: The Development of a Particle Physics Grids." *Information Systems Journal* 21, no. 4 (2011).

Zull, James E. *The Art of Changing the Brain: Enriching Teaching by Exploring the Biology of Learning*, 1st ed. Sterling, VA: Stylus, 2002.

INDEX

ACKNOWLEDGMENTS

If any endeavor requires agility and robust collaboration, communication and coordination, it is the production of a book. Thankfully, I had an embarrassment of riches in this area in the form of many talented and wise colleagues, friends, and professionals who contributed their time and thoughtful insight to help me bring this book to life.

Many of the concepts in this book emerged from my work with clients, workshop participants, and my in-depth study of other organizations that intentionally make the agility shift each day. Without their commitment to agility and generosity in sharing their triumphs and lessons learned this book would not have come to be.

Additional ideas and practices in the book incubated at my creative home among my colleagues and graduate students at DePaul University, School for New Learning, and especially at the Center to Advance Education for Adults. I am grateful for this space to come together with learning and development practitioners and scholars to share and experiment with new ideas and approaches for better learning and development in all settings.

I am also grateful to Laurie Harper whose early encouragement and guidance led me to Bibliomotion, and Paul Strohm for early feedback that helped shape the opening chapters, Amelia Forczak provided masterful editorial support and kept me attuned to the reader's experience at every step.

I am also grateful to my friends and colleagues for their close reading and helpful feedback including Dr. Catherine Marienau, at DePaul University, School for New Learning (SNL), and Tom Barr, advisory board member at the Center to Advance Education for Adults (CAEA) and Knowledge Manager at Enablon, and my friend Michelle Sanford, at the Council for Adult and Experiential Learning (CAEL), and to graphic facilitator, Jill Archer, who mapped many collaborative inquires into learning agility and also developed the image for the Relational Web and agility shift dynamics.

Many thanks to Erika Heilman and Jill Friedlander who lead the team of publishing rock stars at Bibliomotion. It is a joy to work with people who have the capacity to be focused on the details and deadlines while cocreating new ideas. I have been inspired and energized by their entrepreneurial vision throughout the bookmaking process.

Special gratitude and appreciation goes to my "first reader" and partner, Carol Semrad, one of the most agile people I know and whose wisdom, enthusiasm, and support never flag through this or any other adventure.

ABOUT THE AUTHOR

Pamela Meyer, PhD, draws on more than twenty years of organizational development experience to work with clients who want to be more agile and innovative and need new competencies and capacities for strategic success. She helps organizations worldwide work at the top of their capacity, using the strategies she learned in her years building creative teams in the professional theater, combined with innovative strategies from artistic collaboration, and cutting-edge management research and practice.

Pamela is the author of four books on agility, innovation, and learning. In addition to *The Agility Shift*, she is author of *Permission: A Guide to Generating More Ideas, Being More of Yourself and Having More Fun at Work* (Playspace Press, 2011), *From Workplace to Playspace: Innovating, Learning and Changing Through Dynamic Engagement* (Jossey-Bass, 2010) and *Quantum Creativity: Nine Principles to Transform the Way You Work* (McGraw/Contemporary, 2000), as well as numerous articles and papers.

In addition to her work with organizations, Pamela teaches courses in business creativity, organizational change, and adult learning at DePaul University, School for New Learning in Chicago where she is director of the Center to Advance Education for Adults.

When not speaking, consulting, or teaching, Pamela maintains her own agility through amateur ski racing and is a frequent qualifier for the NASTAR championships. To contact Pamela to speak at an event or consult with your organization, visit Pamela-Meyer.com.